¬

# PASTORS AT RISK

## Help for Pastors, Hope for the Church

*Dedicated*
*with affection*
*to*
*the nearly 400,000 pastors*
*across the United States and Canada*
*and their spouses and families*
*and to*
*Beverley London and Bonnie Wiseman,*
*wonderful women of God*
*who know the authors best*
*and who have loved and*
*encouraged them along the way.*

# PASTORS AT RISK

## Help for Pastors, Hope for the Church

# H.B. London, Jr. and Neil B. Wiseman

**VICTOR BOOKS**

A DIVISION OF SCRIPTURE PRESS PUBLICATIONS INC.
USA CANADA ENGLAND

Copyediting: Robert N. Hosack
Cover Design: Joe DeLeon/Paul Higdon

**Library of Congress Cataloging-in-Publication Data**

London, H.B.
  Pastors at risk / by H.B. London, Jr. and Neil B. Wiseman.
    p.    cm.
  Includes bibliographical references.
  ISBN 1-56476-111-8
  1. Clergy — Office. 2. Pastoral theology.   I. Wiseman, Neil B.
II. Title.
BV660.2.L65   1993
253 — dc20
                                            93-3616
                                                CIP

# CONTENTS

I t is impossible to overstate how deeply I feel about the importance of upholding the men and women who serve us through the ministry of the church. They and their families need our support and understanding! H.B. London, Jr. and Neil B. Wiseman are on the cutting edge of a movement that seeks to provide that support. Every concerned and conscientious Christian will want to benefit from their insights.

The pastor has an incredibly significant and difficult job. The implications and ramifications of his responsibilities at church are more extensive than most parishioners realize. A strong church is the first line of defense for healthy families; and healthy families are the building blocks of stable communities. But there's a complicating catch. The pastor, in addition to carrying this heavy responsibility for the church and society, usually has a family of his own at home. All too often time spent in ministry equals time away from spouse and kids. If family stability isn't attacked and eroded at one end of the scale, it seems it will be at the other! This is a serious and delicate situation. And caught in the middle of it all, trying (frantically, sometimes) to keep both ends of the candle burning, is that person we know as the professional minister—a human being like the rest of us, who increasingly finds himself working against a legion of obstacles, unrealistic expectations, and stresses and strains unique to his position in the world.

I have another very personal reason for being concerned about the pastor's family—I grew up in a preacher's home myself! And though my memories of my dad and mom and their tireless dedication to the Lord's work are positive, I do know something about the struggles and hardships encountered by those who serve God's people in that capacity. In spite of a few megachurches and media ministries that make the ministry look like a fairly comfortable calling, the fact remains that, in financial terms, the pastorate is no more promising today than it was when my dad preached his first sermon back in 1935. He received 55 cents as compensation for that initial labor of love, and averaged $8.00 per Sunday for the next fifty-two weeks. His total earnings for that first year in the ministry were $429.82 and, remarkably, he gave $352.00 back to the church. He and my mother lived on a small inheritance that came to them after my grandfather died in 1935 and throughout their lives together gave more than they could afford to the cause of Christ or to anyone who appeared to be more needy than they. Obviously, inflation has jacked up the figures; and yet I'm well aware that many of our pastors today are floundering on the modern equivalent of that $8.00 per week and $429.82 per year. That kind of budgetary restriction just has to place family life under an incredible financial strain!

I am committed, then, to the welfare of pastors and their families. But the question bears even greater significance for society as a whole. For if the pastor's family suffers, the entire church suffers. And if the church fails to be what it should be, society goes a little further adrift. That, I'm convinced, is exactly what we see happening all around us today. Focus on the Family's desire to reach out to pastors where they live is part of our overall plan for building a stronger moral and spiritual foundation for our culture as a whole. This book has arisen out of that concern. The authors are themselves experienced pastors. They know their subject from firsthand experience. H.B. London, Jr. shepherded congregations for three decades before joining the staff of Focus on the Family, the most recent of his charges having been a large and prominent church in Pasadena, California. Neil B. Wiseman has served in a variety of roles—pastor, professor, magazine editor, and currently as academic dean of the Nazarene Bible College in Colorado Springs. Both men can teach us a great deal about strengthening the church and society from the ground up by supporting the people who provide us with spiritual leadership. We think it's sound strategy!

*—Dr. James C. Dobson*
*President, Focus on the Family*

8

## ACKNOWLEDGMENTS

Applause and well-deserved acknowledgment to all who shaped this book—even those who have no idea they were helping.

A sincere salute to contributors—all essential to the effort: Dr. and Mrs. James C. Dobson, whose encouragement and contribution have been invaluable, Dr. Archibald Hart, Gordon and Gail MacDonald, Jerry Bridges, Ron Blue, Linda Riley, Dean Merrill, and Gary Allen.

Thanks to pastors—hardy soul brothers who minister at the front line.

Thanks to pastors' spouses—unsung heroines and heroes of the contemporary church scene.

Thanks to those who shared insights with H.B. Many opened their hearts at conferences in strange places like church aisles, hotel lobbies, or bustling airports. Others taught us much about this book's central message with letters and phone calls to Focus on the Family.

Thanks to second-career students, many new converts in their thirties and forties, from Neil's classes for thought-provoking dialogue that perpetually remolds his outlook on modern ministry.

Thanks to congregations we served over three decades—loving believers who developed us as pastors in places like Salem, Pasadena, Bloomington, Whittier, Moses Lake, Denver, and Pompano Beach.

Thanks to Sue McFadden, H.B.'s secretary, and Pauline Swart, Neil's secretary.

Thanks to other pilgrims of the Way—friends, church leaders, editors, and publishers who are still teaching us, especially Robert Hosack, our efficient editor from Victor Books.

All of you have become praiseworthy commentaries on the grace of God for us.

C ontemporary pastors are caught in frightening spiritual and social tornadoes which are now raging through home, church, community, and culture. No one knows where the next twister might touch down or what values the storms will destroy. As a result, pastors ask themselves, "Does pastoral ministry make any difference in morally turbulent times?"

This book responds with a resounding YES!

Society cannot flourish without godly pastors. How alarming for the Christian cause when men and women of God feel forced to brood about the future of ministry as they watch their work get harder and their world grow more corrupt.

*Something has to be done.* Ministry hazards are choking the hope out of pastors' souls. They feel disenchanted, discouraged, and often even outraged. They question why they should be expected to squander energy on trivial matters when evil threatens to wreck the human race. Fatigue shows in their eyes. Worry slows their stride. And vagueness dulls their preaching.

The church faces a perilous future when pastors find it so tough to survive emotionally and economically. Many flounder for meaning and mission as traditional morality keeps buckling under brutal unrelenting assaults from secular society. For good reason, pastors dread what will be next as the moral Richter scale shoots up to a shocking six most days and sometimes tops ten. Some pastors consider their lives to be shadows of what they dreamed they would be, because many old formulas for ministry no longer work.

*Something has to be done.* Overwork, low pay, and desperation take a terrible toll as pastors struggle to make sense of crammed calendars, hectic homes, splintered dreams, starved intimacy, and shriveled purpose. Some quit in utter hopelessness to sell used cars, hawk Amway, or peddle water softeners. Others lapse into passivity like holy robots. And many of

11

the remaining stouthearted hold on by their fingernails, hoping to find a hidden spring to refresh their weary spirits and scrambled thoughts. No aspect of pastors' lives has been spared, neither personal nor professional.

*Something has to be done.* Just when they are most needed, pastors are going haywire. It is obvious that nothing but vital faith will revive our times and culture. Now more than ever, a disintegrating society needs the spiritual salt that pastors provide.

*Something has to be done.* Pastors are at risk. The risks they face demand an all-out corrective action by the church. All this squandered devotion and wasted talent must be stopped so ministry can be restored to equilibrium and usefulness. Surely God intends pastors to be whole persons — flesh-and-blood examples of how the Gospel works in this kind of a world.

*Something can be done!* As an authentic first step, this book listens meticulously to pastors' anguish, scrutinizes their frustrations, and proposes answers. Though *Pastors at Risk* squarely faces the terrifying hazards, it emphasizes divine enablement and highlights hope. In heartwarming fashion, this book celebrates the grace potential God has built into discipleship, preaching, marriage, counseling, parenting, triumph, vision, leadership, family, and self-worth.

What matters to pastors impacts the work of Christ everywhere. What matters to pastors is important to the authors and publisher of this book. And what matters to pastors shapes congregations and influences clergy families under your roof.

*Pastors at Risk* aims to shout to everyone who will listen that pastors are to be loved and cherished and that they are absolutely essential to the work of God. It intends to remind the entire Christian community that professional ministers are among the most priceless resources God has given the church — without steadfast pastors there can be no vital churches.

*Something pastors can do.* To enjoy a fulfilling future ministry that can transform our culture for Christ, pastors must intentionally move their focus away from trivia to significance. In the process, pastors will be reawakened spiritually and challenged professionally. God always enriches the worker busied with His work.

Effective pastors for the new century must be whole persons who deliberately balance being and doing, family and church, person and profession, worship and work. That means "wounded healers" must allow themselves to be healed through the same Gospel they use to bring recovery and wellness to others. The results: those now victimized by high demands of ministry will become triumphant victors.

Then, as fulfilled disciples of Jesus, this new breed of renewed pastors will develop spiritually robust churches where believers gratifyingly stretch to the full potential of a Christ-quality life. And their vital, fresh ways of being, thinking, doing, and relating will resuscitate dying churches and rejuvenate lethargic congregations.

Then, like bees are attracted to spring flowers, people will be drawn to spiritual leaders who are growing in Christlikeness themselves. To pastors, such a ministry will be brimful of meaning because it is continually energized by intimate friendship with the Lord. And in spite of every hindrance hell can produce, the churches led by these pastors will thrive beyond anyone's most cherished dreams.

As writers of *Pastors at Risk,* we strongly believe God intends ministerial leaders of local churches to be righteous change agents in a confused world. We believe that a robust commitment to Christ thrives inside pastors and that many are fatigued by long-term faithfulness. We think every pastor in North America, regardless of denomination or size of church, has potential to be a Gospel revolutionary at this present moment in time.

The thesis of this book is that (1) pastors' personal growth must be accelerated and (2) their families must be strengthened so they can meet the spiritual needs of the masses in a changed and changing world.

This book summons pastors everywhere to regain wholehearted adventure in ministry as they draw closer to the Source, implement Scripture more dynamically in countless expressions of ministry, serve downcast people, and more accurately exegete the world around them.

Most of the guidance offered in this book came from pastors or their close friends and spouses. These concepts have been pondered, discussed, preached, and taught by the authors in many forums and in many places. We don't offer easy answers, but time-tested and people-tested insights that give real hope to pastors and help to the church.

### Let's Get Acquainted

We are two veteran pastors who feel compelled to write *Pastors at Risk.* We are deeply distressed by the present pain so many colleagues are experiencing in pastoral assignments. Thus, after years of working with ministers, mostly in the trenches, we want to help stay the course and see adventure restored to ministry.

Both of us love pastors and deeply believe that authentic spiritual issues are solved through the front-line ministry of parish churches. We both continue as "pastors in residence" in non-parish settings where we try to view the church through wider lens than we could while serving local congregations.

**Meet H.B. London, Jr.:** H.B. serves the Christian community as Assistant to President Dr. James C. Dobson at Focus on the Family in Colorado Springs. After thirty-one years of pastoring all sized congregations, including his last church of 3,400 members, he founded and continues to direct a vigorous ministry to pastors through Focus on the Family.

London serves and inspires pastors and their families through extensive correspondence and continuous phone contacts, audio and print resource production, a rigorous speaking schedule that takes him to pastors' gatherings around the world, and liaison contacts with Christian radio stations.

Above all else, H.B. London, Jr. is a friend to pastors, and thousands of ministers are practically resourced by his multifaceted ministry at Focus on the Family.

**Meet Neil B. Wiseman:** Neil equips second-career adults for ministry as Academic Dean at Nazarene Bible College, also in Colorado Springs. He believes that his classroom teaching energizes his administrative responsibilities. He multiplies his ministry through hundreds of former students who have been in his pastoral development classes. He has pastored congregations for twenty years and counts his Pompano Beach, Florida pastorate as his "sweetheart" church.

He has written or edited ten books including *Spirituality: God's Rx for Stress*, published in 1992. His ministerial development endeavors include editorship of a church growth quarterly entitled *GROW*, and he directs the Small Church Institute for his denomination. He has been professionally and spiritually committed to pastoral development and renewal for many years.

## Flesh and Blood Sources

Books are often written at quiet mountain retreats or by soothing seashores to allow authors time to ponder and polish *their* ideas. This book, however, is significantly different. It is

15

not simply a book of *our* ideas and concerns, but more of a community effort. It is made up of living sources who serve at the cutting edge of ministry.

Some of the most-respected Christian leaders from around the country have given permission to use their interviews from the *Pastor to Pastor* bimonthly audiocassette program produced by Focus on the Family.

Even closer to the front lines, however, it discusses questions and concerns from pastors' and spouses' letters to H.B. London, Jr. at Focus on the Family. This is a living book dealing with critical issues. Real people are at risk, and we have discovered that there is a lot of hurt out there. Though we are discussing real people and true situations, every attempt has been made to conceal identities, so names have been changed and locations disguised; but the problems are real—critical, shocking, and staggering.

## Our Audience
*Pastors at Risk* is purposefully intended for male pastors and views parish life mostly from a masculine point of view; more than 90 percent of all pastors are male. Our approach in no way denies or even slightly diminishes the fact that many churches are well-served by female pastors. A similar book should be written for women in parish ministry. Thanks to our female readers for your understanding. We hope as you too read this book that you will be patient with our male pronouns and illustrations.

## Let's Renew Ministry Together
The goal of this book is to stimulate personal renewal and spiritual restoration among pastors everywhere. We believe the viable survival of the Christian church depends on the spiritual vigor and devoted labors of present-day pastors.

As we came to the end of the writing, we did what you are about to do. With a yellow highlighter in hand, we read the book through as we sipped coffee and iced tea.

We tried to make every sentence a summons, every paragraph an open door, every page an affirmation, and every conclusion a refreshing word of grace.

We admit we smiled at the right places. We acknowledge that pastors are the reason we wrote. We hope you will find vitality and resolve as you read. But as we finished we also prayed—we prayed for you, we prayed for ourselves, and we prayed for the church that we might all find spiritual grit and supernatural energy to be what the world needs pastors to be.

Straight ahead. Thanks for allowing us into the center of your world for a little while.

—H.B. London, Jr. and Neil B. Wiseman

# PART

ONE

# Comprehending
# the Risks

ONE

# The Current Crises in Pastoral Ministry

A Conversation between Dr. James C. Dobson and H.B. London, Jr.

I f pastors across the land are at such critical risk, how can they be helped?

As an answer to that question, a much-needed ministry for pastors and their families started with a casual conversation between James C. Dobson and H.B. London, Jr. during a family gathering. These Christian pacesetters recognized an urgent need for someone to become "a pastor to pastors" to help ministry professionals cope with the unique stresses they live under. They sensed a need for someone to "plead the cause" of pastors and families to parishioners across North America.

Dr. James C. Dobson is founder and president of Focus on the Family, and Rev. H.B. London, Jr. is a thirty-one-year veteran pastor—most recently serving at the First Church of the Nazarene, Pasadena, California. As first cousins and only sons of ministers, Jim and H.B. were born just nine months apart; they have been close friends since boyhood and were college competitors in sports, dating, and student elections.

As soul friends to hundreds of pastors, Dobson and London are immensely interested in the spiritual health and emotional wellness of pastors and their families everywhere. Their inspired assumption: if the pastor's family is helped, they will in turn multiply ministry to families in their church.

That casual conversation in Dobson's den led to prayer and thoughtful discussions about how Focus on the Family might respond to the unique needs of pastors now serving 350,000 churches across the United States.

The outcome is an innovative commitment by Focus on the Family—headed by H.B. London, Jr.—to assist pastors who face the difficult daily dilemma of meeting the needs of their families while trying to be faithful to the obligations of a contemporary pastorate.

To help pastors build healthier homes, Focus on the Family offers a compassionate heart that seeks to understand their unique stresses; a non-condemning listening "other" for ministers and spouses; and topflight strategies and imaginative resources for spiritual renewal, family life strengthening, time management, and financial stability.

More than 1,900 radio stations worldwide carried the following "Focus on the Family" interview in which Dobson and London discussed the current crises in pastoral ministry. Their conversation shows that building awareness among pastors and lay church leaders is the first step in untangling some of the stress.

**Dobson:** H.B., I believe the church is the first line of defense for the family. It must not be permitted to flounder. It is more important than parachurch ministries like Focus on the Family. But since the local pastor is the most visual one who represents the church, he carries most of the load.

He is the one people call—not Jim Dobson—when they have a family emergency in the middle of the night. He is the one who puts his arm around a person's shoulder to offer comfort in crises and spiritual support when it is needed the most. His role is vital. His work is absolutely essential in our society.

Unfortunately, few people stop to think about how much difficulty, how much depression, and how many obstacles he faces to serve in this way.

**London:** That's right, Jim. In many vital ways, the first line of defense for the family is the church. But it can only be strong when the pastor is emotionally stable and spiritually solid. That is why I believe that if we can strengthen pastors and their families, we can be a catalyst for spiritual renewal in many churches and in the nation. But it is an uphill battle at a time when pastors live in this present cultural paradox of increased religiosity and decreased morality. Pastors have never had to work harder to serve people than they do now. The pressures are incredible and brutal.

**Dobson:** Summarize for us just how healthy pastors' families are today.

**London:** Since there are 350,000 churches in the United States served by pastors who head families, I assume that is the size of our problem. Family groups living in ministers' homes face all the pressures every contemporary family faces plus the unique demands pastoral ministry makes on them. These pastors need help with their families fully as much as they need to be able to do ministry well.

Sure, everyone hears about a few ministers who, because of a moral lapse, commit sexual sin or abscond with God's money. They are counterfeits and embarrass everyone. Though they require rescue, they are not the dominant focus of my concern.

I want to encourage faithful pastors. I want to serve those with deeply felt spiritual commitments who give themselves every hour of every day to ministry. I want to help those ministers whose families sacrifice to keep their husband or father in the pastorate. Those families are the salt of the earth. The church could not exist without them. Those faithful people need help.

**Dobson:** What are the main difficulties the average pastor faces?

**London:** Their most pressing problems relate to time, money, and family. The issues are incredible—almost unbelievable.

**Dobson:** There is a lot of unresolved anguish and pain in that list. What can be done to lift some of these awful burdens?

**London:** For a start, I think we must help pastors balance family and ministry. Balance is the principal issue; everyone wants it but few seem able to make it work for them. They ask, "How do I minister effectively to my family and still be fair to my congregation?" There is always more to do than time allows.

**Dobson:** It's a bottomless pit—they never get done. The burden of unfinished work is probably greater in the pastorate than in any other vocation. But this balance question is a family issue in most occupations.

**London:** The terrible tyranny of the unfinished is always with them. Jim, I have admired you for preaching balance for all the years you have been with Focus on the Family. But like all strong family units, pastors' families need to make it specific—they need to stop and talk to each other, to take time to understand what is happening in each other's lives, to be friends. Then if something is amiss, they need to take time to fix it.

---

## RISK FACTORS

Consider the following sobering survey results of the personal and professional lives of the clergy:

- 90% of pastors work more than 46 hours a week
- 80% believed that pastoral ministry affected their families negatively
- 33% said that being in ministry was an outright hazard to their family
- 75% reported a significant stress-related crisis at least once in their ministry
- 50% felt unable to meet the needs of the job
- 90% felt they were inadequately trained to cope with ministry demands
- 70% say they have a lower self-esteem now than when they started out
- 40% reported a serious conflict with a parishioner at least once a month
- 37% confessed having been involved in inappropriate sexual behavior with someone in the church
- 70% do not have someone they consider a close friend

*1991 Survey of Pastors,*
Fuller Institute of Church Growth

---

22

**Dobson:** H.B., I have been watching your pastoral style for years. I don't think you ever turned down a request for a wedding, a funeral, or a baby dedication, did you? I think I remember your having three or four weddings in one weekend. How did you do it all and keep up with the counseling, hospital calling, and sermon preparation?

**London:** I believe a pastor must take care of his sheep no matter how many he has. Demands in smaller churches, however, may be just as pressing because those pastors serve people who have crises too, and they do not have a large staff of associates as I have had for the last twenty years.

**Dobson:** That means 3:00 in the morning. If someone has a heart attack, you go to the hospital. If someone has a serious automobile accident, you go. And if a family has a runaway teenager, you go to offer support in any possible way.

**London:** That's it exactly. You answer the phone. You get up. You stagger into the shower. You go. You pray all the way. You minster however you can for as long as you are needed. Then you pick up your day wherever you can find it. Many think the shepherd model for pastoring is passé, but it was the model that worked for me.

**Dobson:** How did you develop these concepts of ministry?

**London:** I do not want to sound noble, but I never could figure out another way to do ministry. Availability at the time of need is the name of the game. When trouble comes, the parishioner wants the pastor because of whom he represents—the Living Christ.

I like to think my style comes completely from a pastor's heart. But both of us came from a ministry-saturated family. My grandfather and grandmother on both sides all gave themselves totally to ministry. My dad was always on the go—preaching and teaching and ministering. And when we lived in St. Louis, my mother made 100 house calls a week.

**Dobson:** But that pace takes a terrific toll—emotionally and spiritually, even physically. Faithful ministers must live in a perpetual state of fatigue. Did you ever feel totally burned out like you could not put another foot in front of the other?

London: Many times. Though I do not like to admit it, there were long periods when I didn't take a day off. But that was wrong. I now believe it is a sin against self and family.

Dobson: I laughed many times about how you even sweated about the weather on weekends. As I remember, you were depressed if it rained on Saturday. Since you were my pastor for several years, I know you were totally committed to the church. And many people admired you for it.

London: I started ministry in an era when if you did not have ten more than last Sunday, you were a failure. At least I felt that way. I remember coming home one day and hearing my wife Beverly say, "There is no way we can live this way. You are not being fair to your sons, you are not being fair to me, and you are not being fair to God. Something has to change."

Something has to change—that is the same message I am hearing often these days from the letters pastors write about their frustrations in ministry.

Dobson: Let's talk about what your mail says. When you first came to Focus on the Family I think you wrote 5,000 pastors to see what they were thinking and feeling.

London: Yes, we randomly selected 5,000 pastors from our mailing list of 77,000. We asked three questions:

(1) What is the greatest danger facing pastors and their families today?

(2) What is your number one challenge as you serve your congregation?

(3) If it were possible for me to do so, how could I personally assist you through utilizing the resources of Focus on the Family?

Dobson: What a list of questions. I guess you had a blizzard of responses and the phones started to ring. What conclusions have you reached after reading hundreds of letters?

London: Second to the balance issue is the difficulty of motivating people to live consistent lives and to help the church accomplish the Great Commission. Pastors are frustrated because people seem apathetic. They are experiencing a lack of people who are willing to do acts of Christian service.

I do not want to unfairly overgeneralize, but they indicate that good people seem centered on their own comforts, achievements, and happiness rather than on the needs of others. Of course, the laity have many of the same pressures pastors have in their families and on their jobs.

Dobson: Did you say about 40 percent of pastors say they have considered leaving their pastorates in the last three months?

London: That's what our surveys indicate. And though most of them will never leave the ministry, it does reflect an agonizing dissatisfaction that is largely unrecognized by those outside the profession.

Dobson: That's frightening when you calculate how important the church is to the family, the community, and society in general. The church is the essence of the Christian movement and the cornerstone of everything we believe and stand for. Yet 40 percent of her leaders say they are thinking about bailing out. Why are 40 percent ready to give up?

London: It is a buildup—an overload or even a soul-breaking accumulation—of all we have been discussing. Pastors feel victimized because the work is harder and more complicated than ever before. They work harder now and see less response and fewer results.

People are easily enticed by cultural non-values, so we find people even in the church who place more value on success and show than on spiritual reality and wholehearted repentance and authentic holy living.

There is also a growing mind-set among pastors of all sized churches that makes them feel pressured, or it may even be envy to be like the megachurches. For most, it is an impossible dream, but they hear about it often and some of their church members talk about it often.

Then too I think there is a disheartening message that trickles down from the superchurches through books, tapes, conferences, and religious TV programs so pastors want to be like the biggest churches. But that creates unbelievable frustration because they can't be like the megachurches.

The realities are that most pastors will never pastor churches of more than 100 members. Somehow pastors need to be told that it is pleasing to God and important to the kingdom if they do their work well in whatever size church they serve.

**Dobson:** I realize my qualifications to speak on some of these issues are limited, but I believe an emphasis on numbers is mistaken. It is upside down. The priority is wrong. Put the spiritual needs of people first, and numerical increase will be the natural outgrowth.

**London:** But some small churches have neither quality ministry to people nor increased numbers; some have not had a visitor in church in months or maybe even years. It's hard for a pastor to keep his morale up in those situations.

It is also easy for all of us to forget that the small church is the backbone of the Christian ministry in North America and probably everywhere in the world. There are ten or maybe fifteen churches of 100 or fewer in many communities who are making a significant impact on the corner of the world which God has given them.

**Dobson:** What about the health of those churches? I think I saw a statistic that 90 percent of the churches are in a "survival mode." In other words, they are hanging on for dear life and trying to make ends meet. Do you agree?

**London:** Yes, and many of those churches have tried everything they can think of to do. But they have failed, and they sometimes change pastors every three or four years. They are frustrated by nonproductive activity and tired of preaching that judges their spiritual commitments. And we need to be aware that the secularization of society wounds them greatly because it encourages sporadic attendance and irregular giving.

**Dobson:** That constant moving tears up pastors families too.

**London:** Sure, and they can't even begin to develop trust between pastor and congregation in such a short time — to say nothing about trust in the community for the church.

**Dobson:** And did you tell me more than half of the pastors' wives are severely depressed?

**London:** Yes. And their wives have reason to be depressed in many situations. They are expected not to express themselves about anything. They are supposed to sit in the corner while their husbands run the show. And they die by inches when they see their husbands come home, sit in a chair, and stare into space. They ask, "Is it worth it all? Are we doing any good? Does anyone care? Will it ever change?" And most of the obvious answers are even more frightening than the questions.

**Dobson:** H.B., I have to admit that you are giving me a new perspective on the local congregation and how much the pastorate has changed. I also have to admit that I am a little convicted in the way I deal with pastors from this studio. I have often asked why isn't the church fighting abortion and pornography, and why isn't the church reaching out to single mothers. Now I see that many pastors are hanging on by a thread. It changes my perspective and makes me believe something has to be done to change these situations.

**London:** Jim, I hear you speak often about pastors having full plates. That word picture is amazingly accurate. Their plates are running over with so many demands and causes until they just throw up their hands when a new one comes along. One more challenge to take up a new cause, however noble, is just too much for them. Any additional expectation nearly pushes them over the edge.

**Dobson:** I can see that more clearly now.

**London:** One pastor talks about the wagon with the wheels coming off after the toggle pin was removed from the axles. If I remember right, when the wheels come off the wagon, it either turns over or ends up in the ditch. That illustrates what many pastors feel today.

**Dobson:** How widespread is this problem, and what can be done?

**London:** All I can say is read my mail, answer my phone, hear what pastors tell me in conferences, and then you know pastors are in pain—everywhere. More than anything else they need the love, encouragement, and prayer support of the people they serve.

That is why I believe our mandate is to encourage spiritual restoration and renewal and then help pastors better manage their time, money, and personal lives.

**Dobson:** H.B., you are going to have your hands full with this ministry to pastors. You already do with 77,000 pastors on our mailing list and many others who listen to the radio program but have never asked to be on the mailing list. You can't touch that many lives, but we are going to spread it as far as we can.

**London:** We are going to do it in every possible way. We welcome help from everyone who feels the burden. I think our first responsibility is to initiate spiritual renewal and restoration in the life of the pastor's family. We are going to do it every way we can—through books, tapes, magazines, pastors' gatherings, and conferences.

**Dobson:** It will grow beyond anything you can imagine. Already the phone is ringing off the hook. The Lord brought you here. We are going to make a difference. Do you have a closing word?

**28**

**London**: In the years I have left, I want to be available to speak with pastors and help them extend their ministries to families—especially their own families. I also want to be able to help those who are burned out or depressed. I want pastors the world over to feel loved and valued.

*     *     *

The prevailing crisis among pastors is crystal clear. Contemporary spiritual leaders are under a two-fold assault—one within and one without.

On the inside of the church, many believers have succumbed to the snares of secularism. Pastors deal daily with diluted dedication, family disintegration, superficial commitments, and an accepted churchly consumerism no longer interested in sacrifice, suffering, or servanthood. Well-worn, friendly old words are still used, but the new meanings refer to a Jesus who provides comfortable happiness and makes no demand on conduct or money. Without our realizing it, the enemy has secularized the church without a shot being fired by anyone.

Outside the church, pastors face a new dark age[1] where the masses have no Christian memory, success is king, and faith issues are far down the average person's priority list after the PTA meeting, latest video release, Little League game, or weekend diversion. The secular masses simply do not see the point. Even though they are sometimes magnanimous toward pastors, they really think ministers are wasting their lives for an absurd cause.

However, a penetrating insight from Charles Colson lights a hopeful sunrise in this dark night, "History pivots on the actions of individuals, both great and ordinary."[2] If Colson is right, then every pastor needs to hear and heed the ancient question asked of Queen Esther, "Who knows but whether you have not come to the kingdom for such a time as this?" (Esther 4:14, RSV)

Who knows? God knows. Every individual pastor makes a difference; the *church* and the *world* need every pastor serving at their best for such a time as this.

**29**

# Why Is Ministry
# So Tough Today?

"No one gives our church first priority but me. And it is sometimes hard for me. What is ministry coming to anyway?" – a pastor from Minnesota

P astoring is harder now than ever before. Unprecedented shifts in moral, social, and economic conditions are jolting congregations and bringing into question the way ministry is done. These changing circumstances and values directly affect pastors and their way of life. Many pressing contemporary difficulties were largely unknown in earlier periods of Christian history. Change seems to be in the driver's seat in today's culture and the church.

At the same time, pastors' concepts of ministry are in flux. Now, personal fulfillment and meaning are routinely expected where former generations seemed satisfied with sacrifice and suffering. Current research findings support the conclusion that 80 percent of practicing pastors think ministry negatively affects them or their families.[1] Clearly, this new breed of pastors view their world, their work, and themselves differently than their preaching fathers and grandfathers did. As pastors and lay leaders shift through the fallout of these changes, an inescapable modification of assumptions seems to be underway.

Why Is Ministry So Tough Today?

At the same time, contemporary people, the bedrock reason for ministry, are harder to reach. Americans' preferences and values are shifting more swiftly and profoundly than at any time since the rugged agrarian and individualistic ideals of the early pioneers and settlers.

Religious pollster George Barna summarizes the new realities: "Overwhelmed by information, rocked by innumerable opportunities and a limited number of hours, and struggling to remain abreast of the sweeping changes that are impacting lifestyles and relationships, a substantial number of adults are adopting nontraditional perspectives on some fundamental realities of life. These realities relate to their spiritual perspectives, their views about people, and even their understanding of the reasons for life."[2] How different this synopsis sounds from our traditional views about those we seek to serve in ministry.

As a result, a confusing bewilderment, or maybe downright disorientation about ministry, is being heard across the whole religious spectrum. Listen to the shrinking satisfaction and the desperate panic in what pastors say.

While discussing pastors under his supervision, one church leader said, "Morale is at an all-time low in our geographic area; so many people have lost their jobs and moved away that our pastors are working harder than ever and showing smaller gains."

A third-year seminary student questions if investing his future in service through the church is "good stewardship of life."

Pastors who check the polls are worried about parishioners and prospects. Recent surveys reveal nearly half of all adults (47 percent) agree that the Christian faith is relevant to life, but only slightly more than one quarter (28 percent) think churches in their area are relevant.[3] That is not encouraging news for the church or pastors.

Fear shows in a pastor's voice as he tries to accept the prevailing challenges, "The work is harder than ever before, but the difficulties mean they need us more. Long term, I hope that makes the difficulties beneficial to us."

Surprisingly, in spite of these challenges, many second-career couples still leave stable salaries, comfortable homes, and extended families to train for ministry. Their call may eventually take them to a decaying North American city. Or their first assignment could be in rural America.

However, to get an understandable focus on what many pastors consider to be a lethal professional and spiritual war zone, it is necessary to carefully scrutinize the hazards that dishearten pastors. A useful first step in disarming these frustrations is to comprehend the threats and their origins. Then in response, informed strategies can be designed to meet these rigorous demands.

Someone accurately suggested, "The church is beyond change—what she needs is intentional revolution." Perhaps pastors need to view the church like that too. When they do, the message becomes, "Ministry today is vastly different from what it has traditionally been, so pastors must revitalize their ministry and design strategies to effectively meet contemporary challenges."

## Hazard 1: Walk-on-the-Water Syndrome

Far different from earlier in this century, the man of God is viewed as a kind of third sex—out of touch with the real world. Every minister has his own story about a friendly stranger in the next seat on a plane who stops talking when he learns his fellow traveler is a pastor. Most pastors have been served by a waitress who puts a spiritual spin on the conversation when she learns her customer is a preacher. Conversation at other times shuts down completely when a minister walks up as someone warns, "Clean up your act; the pastor is here."

H.B. experienced the walk-on-the-water syndrome vividly during the ten-speed bicycle craze of a few years back. The church college department bought H.B. a bright orange Schwinn™ ten-speed which almost glowed in the dark. His sons Brad and Byron, aged fifteen and twelve, were so excited they begged, "Dad, come home and go bike riding with us so you can use your new ten-speed."

So H.B. dropped his work, went home, put on his sweatshirt, shorts, tennis shoes, and took off with his overjoyed sons. As they neared home after a fun-filled ride, a red Toyota pickup driven by their next-door neighbor made an abrupt turn in front of the inexperienced pastor/rider. H.B. reached for the nonexistent foot brake; then his hand slipped off the handlebar brake, and he went crashing into the truck. The orange bike crumpled into a mass of spokes and steel; H.B. hit his head, skinned his shins, and bloodied his forehead.

His sons immediately began acting like Secret Service agents, checking every house and vehicle hoping no one saw their dad on the ground.

The nervous driver inquired as he came around the back of his truck, "Are you okay?"

H.B. responded, "Are you kidding? I'm in pain. My bike is broken. My kids are embarrassed. And besides that, why didn't you signal?"

The environment changed radically and the embarrassment increased when the driver's wife came out of her house screaming, "Pastor, pastor, pastor." Then she stuck a bony finger under the driver's nose and said, "See there. You couldn't just hit a kid. You had to hit a pastor."

H.B. finishes the story as he describes how the walk-on-the-water syndrome feels, "I always knew people thought I was different, but I never realized there was a distinct grouping even when you have an accident."

This ministerial mystique makes pastors feel ill at ease. And though laypersons may not realize it, pastors have accidents, eat at McDonalds™, father children, fret about bills, and misunderstand their kids. Some even worry about their own shaky marriages and feel worn down by ministry. No holy aura makes them perfect or even extraordinary, and they know it.

However, the walk-on-the-water syndrome triggers in a

small minority of pastors an obnoxious pseudo-holy opinion of themselves. They begin to believe all the nice things parishioners say about them. They think they can do no wrong. They resist accountability and think they deserve every privilege they can manipulate. But the Apostle Peter left a dazzling warning to such egoists—anyone who tries to walk on water either drowns or swallows large amounts of water.

To find satisfying effectiveness, a pastor's view of himself and his ministry must resist the delusive mirages from both the past and present culture. He must cultivate an accurate awareness of contemporary realities about his environment and about himself.

## Hazard 2: Disastrous Personal Problems
Everyday's mail to H.B.'s office from pastors brings heartbreaking letters. Their writing details the consequences of secret sins, outlines emotional brokenness, and portrays stress which one described as "an inside boiling that feels like I swallowed burning sulfur."

Pastors are also terrified by ministry environments that are changing quicker than anyone can grasp or process. Such environmental changes are like a gigantic iceberg, where individual pastors see only a tiny tip of the far-reaching menace. Overwhelmed, they often feel isolated and guilty when misery comes. Meanwhile, theological educators and church leaders are just as puzzled as the troops in the trenches. Whatever the causes, this unholy holocaust has to be halted.

Consider what pastors think about work, home, and lifestyles as reported in a recent survey conducted by *Leadership* magazine:

- 94 percent feel pressured to have an ideal family;
- The top four problems in clergy marriages are: 81 percent, insufficient time; 71 percent, use of money; 70 percent, income level; 64 percent, communication difficulties, 63 percent, congregational expectations; and 57 percent, differences over leisure;

- 24 percent have received or are receiving marital counseling;
- 33 percent of pastors are dissatisfied with the level of sexual intimacy in their marriages; and pastors report 16 percent of their spouses are dissatisfied, which 69 percent blame on their busy schedule, 54 percent on their spouse's schedule, and 35 percent on frequent night church meetings;
- 22 percent seek supplemental income to make ends meet;
- 28 percent feel current compensation is inadequate;
- 69 percent of the spouses work outside the home to make ends meet;
- 67 percent of the pastors feel positive about their spouses working outside their home;
- 9 percent of clergy have had extramarital affairs;
- 19 percent have had inappropriate sexual contact with another person other than their spouse;
- 55 percent of clergy have no one with whom they can discuss their sexual temptations.[4]

Being forced to deal with this long list of terrorizing issues would create gigantic casualties in any occupational group. Pastors are no different. And the problem is multiplied by a kind of snowballing synergism because no hazard causes difficulty independently of all other problems. Thus, an unsatisfactory reaction in one area significantly impacts other aspects of a pastor's life and ministry.

Then too a domino effect connects difficulties between pastors. In some small but significant way, a downfall by one pastor negatively impacts all ministers and all ministries.

## Hazard 3: Church Member Migration
The history of the church has never seen a phenomenon like the contemporary "member migration." Like wild geese, church members are on the move—not leaving the church, just moving to another local congregation. This superficial

35

loyalty puts pastors among the most vocationally thwarted people in the world. Today, long-held assumptions about doctrinal devotion and congregational commitments no longer apply. Fewer and fewer people choose a church or continue to attend because of biblical teaching or particular tradition. And apparently faithful members might move any day without much warning.

Member migration is a national problem that reaches across denominational boundaries. So in spite of the combined efforts of all churches to win new converts, it is estimated that 80 percent of church growth in recent years is a result of people moving from one church to another.

This migration causes substantial membership losses in mainline churches. It means thousands of smaller churches of various affiliations lose members in droves to larger, multiple-program churches. And denominational labels seem to make little difference in these choices.

The migration works to the advantage of megachurches. Such explosive growth churches, sometimes called "seeker-sensitive," generally emphasize the worshiper rather than God, theology, or ritual. Their public worship includes lots of contemporary music, usually without a hymnal; drama; and sermons organized around felt needs, preached topically and applied to life situations with minimum exegesis of Scripture.

Meanwhile, mainline churches, now somewhat mislabeled, seem to be moving to the sidelines of influence with their severe membership losses. Evangelicals are flocking to megachurches from traditional churches. In the wake of this volatile mobility small churches get smaller, feeding their feelings of inferiority and promoting a survival mentality. In the process, laypeople and ministers who continue in small churches are left to sink or swim as they mourn the losses of members and money.

This displaced-person problem has also increased because of job losses and transfers. When faithful members move to new locations, they leave volunteer ministry assignments vacant. As a result, it may take years to nurture others to replace the loss of even one stable, involved family.

This member migration makes many pastors lose spiritual impetus. Many ministers go to their offices daily more out of a sense of duty than calling, performing tasks with absent vigor. Little happens as they constantly dress old wounds and go through the motions of old routines. They feel frustrated because they do not make a difference. All of this is so unlike the idealism they enjoyed at the beginning of their ministry careers.

These feelings of futility shrink a pastor's soul. At the same time, incentive dries up. It is hard to keep going in a job where little impact is possible, where too much effort is required in too little time, or where no support system helps one to see the value of his work. As a result, many pastors quit trying to lead. They are convinced nothing will happen, and it doesn't.

The loss of relationships in member migration can feed a pastor's vocational depression. Looking at such a situation, examining the limited resources available, evaluating the apparently impossible challenge, and then realizing there is no chance to make a difference is a longhand description of ministerial depression. To say it concisely, spiritual burnout comes from believing there is no reason to try because the situation is always going to be the way it is, or worse.

For the pastor, this debilitating despair undermines his ability to function in his marriage, family, or ministry. In the process, his self-esteem dehydrates. Then to protect his diminishing self-worth, he turns to survival more than outreach. He gives up all expectation of achievement. The limited opportunities and his frame of mind combine to create a treadmill of hopelessness.

Similar conditions in other occupations make people throw life into neutral or bail out of their professions. In light of the pressures, many pastors are settling into sickening monotony or withdrawing from ministry altogether. These grim realities can begin to terrorize a pastor and hypnotize a declining congregation.

## Hazard 4:
## Electronic Technology Shapes Preferences

Videocassettes have now joined top-notch television, audio cassettes, and religious radio to bring the most accomplished preachers, capable musicians, and airbrushed churches into our living rooms and automobiles. Since the masses experience flawless performance firsthand, is it any wonder that church members believe such programs are models of what an exemplary church and effective preacher should be?

Every pastor remembers Sundays when he felt so anointed that he thought no one could exceed his preaching, only to have a worshiper say at the door following his great sermon, "Pastor, did you hear Chuck Swindoll or Robert Schuller this week? What a message!"

The result of this accumulated technological impact is that every pastor must preach to people who often see religious services with jammed sanctuaries, polished musicians, and skilled orators doing their best. By the time parishioners come to church on a Sunday morning, many have already heard magnificent religious music and the most talented preaching in America.

Think of the adjustments members are forced to make when they come to a church of fifty where the air conditioning is broken, the kids are noisy, the music is amateurish, or there is a fly or two buzzing overhead.

No matter how hard they try, these individuals find it nearly impossible not to feel their church is inferior, even though their pastor, after working a full-time second job all week, does his best to open the Word. And it is even worse in situations where the pastor has given up and performs in the maintenance mode only.

In these environments, pastors are victims of technology unlike anything preachers have ever faced. They have no way to come up to the standard created by technology in worship-

**RISK FACTORS**

Less than one half of the people most committed to the church say that their church performs its primary duties with excellence.

George Barna, *What Americans Believe*

ers' minds. Some pastors even preach against the TV preachers as if that would solve anything.

All this results in stiff competition — a word no one wants to use about the church — where the pastor always feels like a loser. Uncertain how to cope with the overwhelmingly demanding dynamics that technology brings, faithful pastors usually push ahead, doing their best and invoking holy words long after optimism is gone and their own souls are starved.

## Hazard 5: People Are More Distracted

Moderns live hectic lives. Laypeople are busier than most pastors realize. Their overstuffed calendars may include daily hours spent in commuter traffic, an acrobatic schedule to allow children to keep staggering school and sports routines, overtime far beyond the traditional forty-hour workweek, workouts at the health club, and jobs that require mother and father to work different shifts. Hundreds of distractions stress them every day.

When average people are bombarded daily by such commitments and diversions, the church becomes just another appendage to modern living. It is no longer the social center of family life it once was. There was a time, that is gone forever, when a carnival or a revival used to capture the attention of a whole town, and one wag said, "You really couldn't tell which it was in many cases."

Such influence is now past. Now, the church has become only another small part of an overbooked schedule. As a result, it is an uphill struggle to get people to attend anything more than one activity per week. And their distractions undercut their stewardship and service.

## Hazard 6: Consumer Mentality

Consumer mentality saturates the American way of life. Shopping malls are centerpieces of community life. Consumers can purchase almost anything whenever they desire. They expect to find an abundant supply of sizes, colors, and prices. These same people naturally want church programs and ministries to appeal to varied interests. Frighteningly, however, they frequently have little commitment to make things happen or to help fund the cost of such a smorgasboard approach to ministry.

This reality means that when people move to a new community, they choose a church on the basis of what it does for them rather than what they can do for it. This is the result of our contemporary focus on self-fulfillment and happiness at any cost. Doctrinal lines have become so blurred that few people choose a church anymore for its biblical teaching or theological soundness.

The consumer mentality also prompts people to change to churches where they can have better children's programs, more appealing music, larger facilities, more convenient parking, more exciting preaching, or more energetic services.

In the church, the consumer mentality is like changing supermarkets or gas stations; the customer simply moves down the street to the next church of his or her choice.

This consumer mentality sometimes causes people to change churches to dodge responsibilities. They do not want to teach Sunday School. They want nothing to do with teenagers. Or they do not want to "baby-sit" in the nursery. They simply want a church which provides inspiration and encouragement for themselves.

Such consumers view the church as a means to achieve their goals of bliss and respectability. They may even feel uncomfortable with the biblical language of sin and salvation. All of this is a subtle secular subversion taking place inside those who claim to be serious followers of the Lord Jesus.

The most pressing question for followers of the consumer mentality is, "What has the church done for me lately?"

## Hazard 7: Suffocating Expectations
Expectations in the church are going up while commitments are going down.

These days, some church members may say straightforwardly, "Pastor, you are paid to do church work, so you unravel the difficulties and care for the details." How ironic that at a time in North America when involvement is viewed as a disposable commodity in so many Christian circles, the church keeps growing so rapidly in parts of the world where it is a lay-driven movement.

Even emotionally robust pastors find it takes lots of energy and large doses of patience to simultaneously cope with whining traditionalists, demanding baby boomers, and lethargic church members. And in times of tight budgets and declining volunteerism, some congregations increase the pastor's burden by expecting him to deal with trivia like folding bulletins and cutting the grass.

As a result, a perpetual pastoral juggling act is required to deal with the mushrooming expectations that originate from spouse, children, congregation, denomination, community, or even self. To jumble the issues even more, these expectations often conflict with each other.

As a result, a dehumanizing fatigue of faithfulness becomes a way of life for too many pastors. Unfinished tasks dog them, so they are never free from omnipresent demands—at dinner, on the basketball court, on days off, or in tender moments with spouse or children. Even the strong feel their stamina wearing thin.

Perhaps a freeing insight comes from Hugh Prather when he suggests expectations are an enslaving judgment we make of each other. He thinks expectations are often so far off the mark of reality or possibility that they drive wedges between people who formerly had fine relationships before one of them got carried away with an impossible ideal. As a solution, he suggests, "Expectations, like cataracts, must be removed because there is no way around them."[5]

Thinking through ways to make Prather's advice a reality is a stimulating exercise for a pastor who feels burdened down with unrealistic expectations from his flock. Amazingly, his expectations of parishioners and his family may be as absurd as their expectations of him. Expectations lock pastor and congregations into dismal relational prisons.

## Hazard 8: Decimated Absolutes

Our permissive society has trashed absolutes. *For sures* have been bartered for *maybes*. Little is being done to repair ethical foundations that are crumbling everywhere. The Ten Commandments have been rejected as the code of conduct in our culture. The U.S. population has increased 41 percent since 1960. "But during that time there has been a 560 percent increase in violent crimes; a 419 percent increase in illegitimate births, a quadrupling in divorce rates; a tripling of the percentage of children living in single parent homes; more than 200 percent increase in teenage suicides; and a drop of almost 80 points in SAT scores."[6] Society may be dying because we have such a short supply of self-control, compassion, tolerance, faith, integrity, and respect for authority.

Today, even believers routinely respond to a "thus saith the Lord" with "I'm not so sure." Laypersons seldom evaluate life by biblical truth their pastor preaches. Church constitutions or creedal statements are viewed as relics out of the past. Everyone does what is right in his own eyes.

Regrettably, this problem is more than a collapse of moral absolutes in society. It also grows out of subtle shifts where clergy and local lay leaders have loosened their commitments to biblical preciseness and holy behavior. In part, this drift probably results from obliging attempts to appeal to the masses and to promote peace among theological traditions.

Whatever the reasons, biblical absolutes have deteriorated into mere opinions. In many seminaries and theological schools, old lines of doctrinal differences have been obscured between conservatives and liberals to the point where debate and controversy are no longer necessary. No absolute standard is embraced or accepted. The salt is losing its saltiness.

**RISK FACTORS**

Two out of three adult Americans (67%) say there is no such thing as absolute truth.

George Barna, *What Americans Believe*

Consequently, many view biblical and doctrinal issues as a theological cafeteria where they choose what truth they want to govern their lives. Thus, many apparently join the church these days by a socializing osmosis rather than as a result of a supernatural character transformation.

The devaluing of virtue and fading moral absolutes makes pastoring difficult and biblically based preaching nearly impossible. In truth, virtue in some circles is considered contaminated because it often keeps company with Christian believers.

## Hazard 9: Money Struggles

Contemporary money problems are forcing churches to radically revise their economic priorities. Giving is down and costs are up. Two paychecks are the norm in most households, including the pastor's. And young pastors often carry staggering educational debts into the morning of their ministry with limited ways to repay them.

Other problems complicate economic issues. The graying of members also means many need ministry well beyond their peak earning and giving years. Middle-income jobs are being eliminated throughout society. And health insurance for everyone, including pastors, has skyrocketed to inconceivable levels.

Studies indicate baby boomers give less to the church and more to other charitable causes. And with downturns in the national and international economies, individual, foundation, corporation, and even government funding have shrunk for charitable, social, and educational causes. There is less money from all sources at a time when needs are increasing and costs are going up.

All these factors impact a pastor's pocketbook. A dropping economy works against a pastor's standard of living because fixed or escalating costs at church make it virtually impossible to increase the pastor's salary, no matter how much he deserves it or how much the church wants to do it. The resulting financial pressures are tough and unmanagable.

Realities show that the older the pastor's family becomes and the longer he goes without a raise, the less he is able to buy basics, to say nothing about keeping up with community economic standards. At the same time, a pastor is usually locked into a middle-class standard of living by his tastes, his education, and his congregation's expectations.

To meet or solve financial burdens, the pastor often becomes bi-vocational or his wife goes to work—sometimes both. In addition, they struggle to find time for children, carpools, and chores. In those situations, the wife often must take employment to help provide essentials for the family. Then, her commitments to the world of work outside her home force her to diminish involvement in the church and vastly hinder the family's ability to move. Consequently, many pastors continue in current pastorates for economic reasons when they should move on. In the struggle of being locked in, they become more weary, lose their challenge, or self-destruct emotionally.

## Hazard 10: Dwindling Public Confidence

The Jim Bakker and Jimmy Swaggart scandals plummeted public trust for ministers to all-time lows. Less prominent but equally offending pastors have also belittled the cause of Christ. In light of these moral breakdowns, pastors should not be surprised that society no longer reveres them as shapers of conscience or communicators of values. Like it or not, millions view ministers as trifling, demagogic, self-seeking, lazy, or even immoral.

As a result, few people seriously listen to what pastors say about anything, especially the meaning of life, faith, morals, or redemption.

All is not futile, however. As hard as it seems, by their own integrity pastors must face these realities and live down these bad reputations. A commitment to a personal quality of Christlikeness gives amazing meaning to the pastor's life and at the same time makes him a powerful example to those he serves.

A pastor's Christ-quality life is God's most convincing answer to secular suspicions of spiritual shepherds.

## Hazard 11: Dysfunctional People

The breakdown of the American home and family has greatly complicated pastoral care and expanded the need for it. No end of dysfunctional family problems is in sight.

A pastor, serving his first church which he describes as an average-sized rural/resort church, summarizes the overloads dysfunctional people cause for pastors: "I spend enormous time rescuing people from their sins—sexual problems of every kind (rape, child abuse, surrogate parenting, shattered marriages, homosexuality, sex education), addictions to drugs and alcohol, addictions to laziness and work, anorexia, anger and rage, stunted personality development, low self-esteem, and hopelessness."

He closes his letter by adding another difficulty most people would not think to consider, "In our county, more than 20 percent of the population receive financial support from social services that have government policies that work against Christian values. Some people who live together do not get married because it would cut their welfare income." Such emotional drains added together leave a pastor little energy to accomplish the more traditional and required functions of ministry.

Now dysfunctional family relationships are so common that a high percentage of individuals in every congregation carry scars from a fractured childhood. They look to the church as their most convenient help. When churches ignore these pains in persons in their fellowship, the unresolved issues pop up in strange and unexpected ways. Like an acre of dandelions, the crop gets worse when ignored.

Fallout from dysfunctional homes accelerates in geometric proportions when persons who go into ministry bring unresolved emotional baggage with them from childhood or earlier pastorates. It has been reported that 80 percent of today's ministers come from dysfunctional families. If accurate, that means many churches have dysfunctional pastors leading a congregation of dysfunctional people. What an explosive mine field!

If pastors do not intentionally resolve their past personal problems, the demands dysfunctional people bring to them will create personal burnout, stress, and depression. Helping dysfunctional people uses up lots of the healer's energy, but it is even harder when the leader has to deal with his own problems at the same time.

Consequently, seasoned pastors are terrified by the personal and family crises they observe in ministerial colleagues. They wonder if ministry harms their children, shortchanges their marriages, or damages their own wholeness. Since they fear what burnout can do, many are reexamining ministry decisions once settled for life. Others desperately try to deal with long-buried emotional difficulties. To make matters worse, they are afraid to go for help because they do not know whom to trust with their inward secrets.

**RISK FACTORS**

12% of ministers reported they were depressed often or always in their ministry.

Blackmon and Hart,
*Clergy Assessment and Career Development*

## Hazard 12: Defection Spirals
Pastoral AWOL is on the increase. Front-line troops desert because they are shocked by secularism on the inside and overwhelmed by chaos on the outside. The problem is so large that church leaders fear not enough battle-ready soldiers will be available to impact the remainder of this decade or the new century. No one can guess what the defection rate will be when the fight becomes more fierce, as it will. And the battle fatigue of those who remain will thwart their productivity.

In this current downgrading of ministers in our society, recruits are baffled because even rudimentary assumptions about ministry apparently fly in the face of present values. And armchair pessimists, even inside the church, goad prospects with queries about how preposterous their occupational plans seem from a commonsense point of view. Accurately, the doubters suggest that ministry requires one to forsake family roots, submit to rigorous training, and commit to lifelong low pay. They argue: Why pay such a high price for a cause which may be losing its soul?

The future of ministry is in crisis because fewer exemplary candidates are answering God's call to ministry. Both the quality and numbers have tapered off.

## Hazard 13: Infidelity Escalates

Each week brings heartbreaking news about another moral failure by a fellow minister. Some say infidelity by pastors is the bottom line of an accumulation of a thousand small things that go wrong in a marriage that no one takes time to fix. When ignored, what seems to be innocuously unimportant flares into a moral or emotional earthquake that ends in episodes of adultery. Could it be that the overly fatigued pastor does not heed the spiritual withering in his own heart?

A menacing caution about spiritual depletion shows in this minister's letter: "Pastors often carry a sense of futility about ministry into their homes when they are not effective in facilitating Spirit-directed, positive change in the lives of those whom they serve. . . . This creates an edginess at home that easily casts a negative shadow on family relationships. The pastor then has a temptation to resent the emotional necessities of his wife and family upon him." On the contrary, he may miss the overwhelming joy and satisfaction they can bring.

Don't miss an important fact: pastors are alarmingly vulnerable to outside emotional support during seasons of frustrating futility. That is why every possible prevention components that flow from a fulfilled marriage must never be permitted to falter.

Whatever the tempting causes, infidelity is sinfully wrong, invariably sabotages the work of God, and destroys redemptive relationships between pastors and their congregations. Every minister is harmed by another's moral bankruptcy. One fallen pastor ruins the credibility of a thousand or more fellow ministers and makes their work immeasurably more difficult. And those closest to the problem in the family or in the local church carry scars forever.

For these reasons and more, every pastor should scrupulously weigh two often overlooked facts: (1) infidelity by one minister hinders the kingdom work and may turn someone from Christ forever, and (2) a happy, satisfying marriage energizes ministry.

Why not renew the existing marriage? To rekindle an old love is a thousand times more sensible and pure than to participate in a scandalous adulterous fling.

## Hazard 14: Leadership Crises

Major institutions from medicine to military to ministry are undergoing a leadership crisis. A wise old pessimist underlines our dilemma, "The problem with our world is that teachers won't teach, presidents won't lead, doctors won't doctor, sales clerks won't sell, and preachers won't preach." In many places, the church is adrift without vision or purpose for want of competent, Christ-centered leaders.

The leadership crisis could be a character issue because rigorous principles of integrity and devoted, distinguished service for the common good have been quietly abandoned. These values have been replaced by a quest for personal privilege and professional advancement. Everybody knows someone who uses the church for personal gain. As a result, we grieve. But perhaps we are too intimidated or frightened to raise a word of protest. And we may be too fooled to face ourselves.

Regardless of his church's size, every pastor is tempted to use power abusively—often every day. An ego craving to be in control—a problem which nauseates pastors in laypeople—is even more poisonous to a pastor. Embers of spiritual vigor are going out in many congregations because there is a civil war for control in progress.

Maybe it is time to recall that the control issue is supposed to be remedied by absolute loyalty to the lordship of Christ, from the least to the greatest.

In terms of the Suffering Servant's viewpoint, it might be a contradiction to call anyone an "executive" or "senior" pastor, to call a bishop or his counterpart a "CEO," or to call oneself "boss" over other team members in a Christian organization. The Apostle Paul's description of a leader is "fellow servant." The Son of God, who considered it a privilege to be called the servant of God and man, must weep over the present climate in many Christian organizations where self-seeking for prominence and power goes on.

The hazards over controling leadership must be changed. Such leadership must be energized by a pastor's personal devotion to Christ, by his creative encounter with biblical truth, and by his efforts to motivate laypeople to implement great causes. Spiritually vigorous and exceptionally enabled individuals are needed to lead the church out of her existing gridlock into a glorious future of holy achievement.

## Hazard 15: Lonely in a Crowd

Loneliness is a growing problem in our culture, especially among pastors. Divorce, transience, and economic displacement create wrenching disruptions of relationships with "significant others." Like a chronic virus, loneliness incapacitates pastors. One pastor said, "Loneliness feels like God is gone and has taken everyone who mattered with Him." Loneliness is an occupational hazard for clergy—though the opposite is often assumed—because so much of their work is done alone behind the scenes like sermon preparation, administrative details, and personal prayer.

Pastoral care can also be lonely business as a minister supports persons in crises, for when he leaves the accident scene, hospital room, or death chamber, the pastor is left alone with his own life-and-death questions for God.

Geographic isolation goes with the territory too, because pastors often reside great distances from their college and seminary classmates, extended families, and childhood friends. Special treatment by laity, though well intended and usually appreciated by clergy, also tends to leave pastors isolated from the common people, so they are never allowed to be human—only "the Reverend."

Another root of loneliness comes from being different, and
the essence of pastoring makes a minister different. Author
Elizabeth Skoglund makes a riveting point that applies to
both laity and pastors: "Interestingly enough, I believe that it is
more the sincere, the thinkers, those who follow hard after God,
who are at times the most lonely in the church. For they are the
ones who question, who disagree, and who will not become blind
sheep following a pope-like leader."[7] All this sounds like any
deviation from any accepted norm may cause loneliness, and
that involves a large part of the Christian enterprise.

Those at the top of an organization also create isolation for
themselves when they assume, "I am better than the people I
serve . . . better than my neighbors . . . better than anyone in
the church. How can I be close to anyone whose opinion I do
not respect or someone who reports to me at work?" Unfortunately, many pastors view parishioners like that.

Many others keep themselves emotionally isolated because
they fear being upstaged. They are troubled that someone
might see their weakness if they get too close. Therefore, they
keep their distance from others because the facts are not as
good as people think. None of this sounds like the relational
patterns of Jesus.

Most pastors have few close friends though parishioners
surround them. How sad, because we all need relationships to
be emotionally and spiritually whole. In the wastelands of ministerial isolation, pastors find easy agreement with Mother Tere-
sa's answer when asked what she thought was the worse disease, "It is not AIDS, leprosy, or cancer, but loneliness."

But it does not have to be that way. Many new friends are
waiting for a small word of permission to walk into their
pastor's heart.

In moments of candid insight, many pastors admit they do
not know how to cultivate friendships. In fact, many think
living in isolation makes them faithful to their training which
taught that friendships were a sacrifice pastors must make to
avoid feelings of jealousy or bias among church members.

How silly! Think again. What whole person is jealous of his

doctor's, lawyer's, or teacher's friends? Still the long perpetuated myth lives on.

Wisdom for living beyond loneliness in ministry can be found in Skoglund's perceptive words: "The solution is not to bury one's feelings in busyness or to run to an exotic resort . . . . [But living beyond loneliness] is to be found in the positiveness of a task and the reality of one's Taskmaster. It is to be found in quietness in one's own backyard. It is not for sale, cannot be bartered for or negotiated. Yet, to live beyond loneliness is a state for which kings would exchange their power and fortunes."[8]

## THE CONTEMPORARY CHALLENGE
### FACE DOWN THE HAZARDS

Friend in ministry, work hard to overcome these hazards. For ministry can be happy work. Keep the long view of Christ in mind and do not succumb to insanities about ministry. Rather, immerse yourself in the graced segments of service for Christ so you rescue people from the enslavements of their sin and help establish them in a Christ-quality life. Immerse yourself in greatness and keep remembering that nothing withstands love.

Remember, the battle is the Lord's. He has called you. He has honored you with a partnership with Him. God's power is greater than anything the world ever throws at your ministry. No weapon in the world's arsenal is a match for God's awesome strength to keep you strong in spite of everything. You are a unique and extraordinary gift of grace God has given to those you have been called to serve. Don't ever forget it.

The enabling spirit of Christ that sets a pastor apart for ministry is the same fuel that makes high-achievement ministry possible, even in tough times.

Confront the hazards with God-enabled courage, creativity, imagination, and faith. What needs to be done must be done. And what needs to be done can be done.

# PART
**TWO**

# Surviving
# the Storm

# THREE

# What Sets the Agenda
# for Ministry?

"Unfair expectations from church people during my childhood made
me resist God's love and grace."—a pastor's daughter from Illinois

P rofessional pastoring has me weary to the bone" is
the way Roger Gendron signaled a cry for help in a
pastor's support group in a small town ninety miles
from Chicago. Four pastors make up the group—a Methodist,
a Baptist, a Roman Catholic, and a charismatic.

Roger persisted, "When I allow expectations to crowd
Christ out of my ministry, I feel devoid of His life-changing
power that should flow through me into my work for God."

Tension mounted in the group as Roger spoke because they
suffered too from ministerial energy depletion. Members of
this group, like most pastors, are harassed by expectations,
especially those that have little to do with ministry.

"Christ crowded out" is slow but certain suicide for ministry. Can expectations really crowd Christ out of ministry?
Whose expectations are worth such a high price? Ministry
without Christ describes the most draining and useless of all
human activity.

Who sets the agenda is the most pivotal issue of modern

ministry. Most ministers have too many bosses and wear too many hats. In too many cases, a pastor is expected to do whatever chore anyone dreams up for him because no one knows exactly what his real job is. That may be the key reason many churches stand still—their pastor is overwhelmed with trivia. He has no time left for what matters most.

This soul-weariness shines through a few lines of sarcasm one minister wrote in his journal: "If I wanted to drive a manager up the wall, I would make him responsible for the success of an organization and give him no authority. I would provide him with unclear goals, not commonly agreed upon by the organization. I would ask him to provide a service of an ill-defined nature, apply a body of knowledge having few absolutes, and staff his organization with only volunteers. I would expect him to work ten to twelve hours per day and have his work evaluated by a committee of 300 to 500 amateurs. I would call him a minister and make him accountable to God."[1]

**Urgent Lessons about Expectations**
A blizzard of letters to H.B. recount mind-boggling confusion about unreal expectations in hundreds of local congregations. Though many pastors seem willing to settle for efforts to balance expectations, others insist they no longer want the job they are educated to do. The distress is painfully real.

• *Salary*—a mission pastor: "It is almost as if the church members resent paying our salary because it competes with things they would like to have for our church. It is only through months of waiting on God that we have stayed in ministry at all."

• *Strain on pastor's marriage*—a minister's wife: "Unrealistic expectations pull the pastor and his wife away from each other and many times hinder their walk with God."

• *Ministry received but nothing given*—a flip side of expectation is a congregation's willingness to take ministry but give nothing in return. Such a situation was described by a pastor from the South Central United States: "It seems that so many of our members are more than willing to have ministries so long as someone else does the job."

• *Burnout blamed on expectations* — a pastor's wife from California: "We wear so many hats. From our family we provide preaching, directing the choir, pianist, special music, Sunday School teachers, bookkeeper, ladies' ministries, and many more. Burnout from sheer physical exhaustion is just around the corner most of the time."

• *Manipulation* — an insightful pastor from Hawaii: "I felt manipulated and guilty when a nonmember who came for spiritual counsel threatened suicide. She intruded on our family time, called at all hours of the night, and made outrageous time demands at the study. She assumed she had a right to do this, and I allowed it because I did not know what else to do."

• *Many things needed for churches to prosper* — a pastor who serves seven rural churches: "A pastor needs to do too many things well in order for the church to prosper, including administration, biblical scholarship, counseling, youth work, and pastoral calling. The results are either a dysfunctional family life or divorce at home."

• *Outreach dissatisfactions* — a pastor's wife from the Northwest: "Our high-energy outreach efforts tend to generate little response. And our leaders blame my husband because the church does not grow."

• *Self-imposed expectations* — a pastor from the Northeast: "Pastors need to set boundaries. The pastor and the people need to realize the pastor does not solve all their problems. Without good perimeters, we take blame when things go wrong even when we had no responsibility in the matter."

• *Counseling misfired* — a pastor's wife from Maine: "My husband is not a bad pastor just because a couple he is working with go ahead with a divorce."

• *My expectations or theirs* — a minister from the Southwest: "I am not sure if the expectations come from the church or from me. Either way, they have the same effect on my sanity and body. How sad if we pastors order our lives by expectations we think the congregation has when we are actually driven by our own inner need to succeed."

• *Self-imposed requirements* — a youth pastor from Sacramento: "I am my own pusher and worst critic. I need to learn to walk with God intimately, invest in my family, and still work hard in ministry. I do not know how to find a balance. Can you help me?"

• *Abused priorities* — a pastor from Michigan: "I abuse priorities and blame it on the church. It is easy to allow ministry demands to make me reschedule family responsibilities. Unfortunately, years sometimes slip by before a pastor sees the error. But I must face the truth that the church would be happy for me to put family at a higher priority. Since I can, why don't I?"

• *Downward spiral of expectations* — consider a portion of this letter where a pastor recaps three crippling backlashes that flow from unbalanced, unrealistic, and unmet expectations:

> There is a downward spiral in unrealistic expectations in a church which harms everyone.
>
> First, the people become passive and dependent. Believing the pastor's education is what qualified him to minister, they quite logically conclude from this erroneous premise that they are unable to minister. The responsibility for ministry, therefore, falls completely on the pastor.
>
> The second step is to see the pastor as a professional who "gets paid for ministering," so they reason, "why should we do his job?" They reason falsely that the responsibility for ministry falls totally on the pastor.
>
> A third destructive attitude springs from their passivity and dependence. Passive, dependent individuals often become demanding people who heap increasing loads of responsibility for ministry on the pastor.

## Judge the Fallout
The preceding observation noting the connection of passive, dependent, and apathetic people with the expectations they

make hits right on target in much of contemporary church life. Uninvolved, demanding people often unknowingly create churchwide discontent at times when the pastor is too fatigued or too fed up to challenge their disruption. As a result, it seems easier to do what is expected than to mop up the crises these people incite. In the process, the pastor becomes a pawn of unrealistic people and his own spirituality stagnates.

Another serious fallout evolves when laypeople or ministers put a professional spin on the pastorate. Even though a pastor, by education and credential, is a true professional, when precise definitions are used, he does his work best when he views himself as a servant of Christ and the people. More influential than a board chairman of the largest corporation can ever be, a faithful pastor can make a life-changing and eternal difference in people's lives.

## Who Decides What Pastors Do?
Where do expectations start? According to one overworked pastor, the answer is "Everywhere and with everyone."

Think how many people are involved in formulating expectations for a pastor's ministry: church members, official documents, colleagues, theological educators, secular literature, ecclesiastical superiors, role models, and even TV talk-show hosts. And in a discussion of the matter a seminary professor added, "Don't forget Jesus and Paul." That many sources make expectations so muddled that even legitimate demands become confusing or downright contradictory.

### Amateurs
Expectations are frequently formed in the minds of well-meaning amateurs who possess limited knowledge of ministry. Though these expectations may be good-natured and intend no harm, they often irritate pastors. Every seasoned minister can recite a long list of things people have expected of him.

A mechanic extends a pseudo compliment following a worship service, "It was a wonderful sermon. I'm glad you have

**57**

that old sermon file where you can grab a good sermon and preach it to us. Pretty soft job, Reverend, working one day a week." The pastor thinks the mechanic means, "I like you, but you sure don't work very hard compared to the rest of us." The pastor is left speechless because he knows he will never change this man's ideas about ministry. For weeks, a flashback of this conversation makes the minister mildly miserable.

Or a retiree murmurs to a fellow church member, "I haven't seen the pastor for a month. I feel like he is neglecting me. What does he do with his time?" When the criticism reaches the pastor, as it will, he thinks the retiree means, "The pastor does not take care of old people like he should." The retiree is really saying, "The pastor is among the most important people in my life, and I count on his attention."

Or a church usher grumbles to a lay leader, "I told the pastor we needed new light bulbs in the hallways, but they are still burned out today." The pastor thinks the usher means, "The minister is responsible for maintenance, and why doesn't he get on the ball and replace the light." The usher, in fact, wanted the lay leader to give higher priority to the church's maintenance needs and take this load off the pastor's mind.

Everyone has definite opinions about what the pastor should do. Many think God has given them a right to see that the pastor knows what they expect and does it. Unfortunately, many unworthy or impossible expectations are passed from one generation to another without much thought or evaluation.

### RISK FACTORS

William Moore in a study of 341 clergy from 36 denominations and 43 states showed that unrealistic expectations are a major factor in pastor burnout.
Malony and Hunt, *The Psychology of Clergy*

*Troubled People*
In today's ministry environment, more than ever before, a new layer of rising expectations comes from troubled people who want something better than broken marriages, dysfunc-

58

tional families, and pagan lifestyles. To their amazement, they discover answers to life's riddles and joy when they turn to Christ. They then view the pastor as the key person in this new relationship with the family of God. Much like combat victims, these wounded, restored pagans require warmth, direction, guidance, conversation, counseling, discipleship, healing, and lots of time. Their needs are monumental and their expectations overwhelming. Inasmuch as the pastor seems willing to befriend them, they sometimes stretch his skills and availability to the breaking point. And when the pastor is not accessible, they feel rejected.

## Family
Highly influential and outspoken formulators of expectations often reside at the pastor's address. His wife and children may not understand why it takes so much time and effort to be a faithful pastor. They ask, Why do you go to work so early in the morning when no one is expecting you? Why did you get home so late last night? Is it necessary to visit sick people in the hospital every day when no one else in the church does it?

## Community
Sources of expectations in the community include civic duties, hospital visitation policy, school activities, social service agencies, and ministerial associations. Though the intensity of involvement varies from one pastorate to another, some degree of strong demand is always present.

## Church Organizational Structures
Local church structures and denominational commitments also contribute to the dilemma. Pastors serving independent churches often have constraining demands of their local congregations shaped by constitutions, traditions, and the views of powerful lay leaders. Conversely, pastors with denominational connections are expected to be involved in the life of their family of churches and to give loyalty to denominational

programs. Both structures need pastors who willingly meet organizational demands. These expectations are real though they may be understated or subtle.

## Personal

Because ministry is a faith issue at its core, pastors must reconcile their call to ministry with what they think God expects in their present assignment. For this reason, much of this exploitation by expectation originates in the pastor's inner world. His wife, church, and children are not the only sources of his confusion. He is often the source of unrealistic demands.

Though pastors may not realize it, ministerial enslavements are sometimes self-induced by a perfectionistic tenacity to do too many things, too often, and too well. This inner problem may be rooted in unrealistic goals for life, for ministry, and for the present setting. Too often the pastor does not face the fact that he is a generalist and not a specialist, which means he will probably not be able to do everything as well as the best he has seen.

Sad but true, his own expectations make a pastor apprehensive about how he spends his time, energy, and money. These annoyances can easily goad pastors to second guess even their best efforts.

Such distractions can make a pastor wonder if his tone of voice in his sermons was sufficiently pastoral. Later, while working at being a good parent, he may experience self-doubt that someone needs him more somewhere else. And during a competent administrative presentation, he can find himself musing about how to arrange the biggest wedding of the year or about someone with a terminal illness.

Many enslaving expectations are self-induced.

## Inner Agitator

Claiming to be a trusted confidant, the *inner agitator* is actually an inner antagonist—an accuser—who arouses fears of failure, reminds of unfulfilled obligations, and saturates thoughts with blame. Like a critical prompter in a play, the inner agitator tries night and day to correct every real and imaginary fault.

This inner agitator holds the pastor hostage, presents itself as an enlightened conscience and sometimes claims to speak for God. A preacher friend calls this harsh companion a *taskmaster within* who drives him like a slave before the Emancipation Proclamation. The resulting bondage produces a dismal ministry.

More often than not, the inner agitator holds the pastor captive to a truckload of accumulated expectations from his past that have little to do with his present assignment. In this buildup, the pastor should be aware that he is dealing with an accumulation that did not originate from one congregation, one church leader, or even a handful of people in the local church. The pastor needs to throttle this inner agitator so he does not blame all his conundrums about expectations on the present congregation. His present concerns may have started half a lifetime ago by someone who has been in the cemetery for years. The heartbreak is the pastor or spouse who is riveted on issues that no one in the present setting cares about. How sad to fight such unnecessary battles in the soul.

## Expectations Hypnotize Pastors

Actual or assumed expectations smother vitality out of a pastor's spirit. Then what "they" think or what "they" want tortures him with bad scenarios of what might happen. As a result, disquieting fears nag every expression of ministry, and pastors become so spoofed they cannot see the difference between a pesky mosquito and a ferocious lion.

These occupational hazards extend into every dimension of a pastor's life, including his home. Right or wrong, pastors often believe the community and church expect them to be a perfect family. This bafflement shows in the comment, "Our church has the stereotypical belief that pastors' kids are going to be the worst or the best. Ours do not measure up either way."

A pastor's wife summarizes this strain: "It seems everyone

**61**

wants to have a piece of us and of our time. It is smothering us." And another pastor speaking about the family identity question observes, "My wife struggles to be seen as Sue and not like the last pastor's wife." Vision and vitality are strangled to death by these strains.

Without extreme care, these debilitating feelings shut a pastor off from two energizing forces for ministry—intimacy with Christ and tenderness with family. A mature minister warns: "In the overload frame of mind, a pastor often gives up on a fruitful devotional life and a robust, satisfying family life. As a consequence, many wrestle with empty souls and a loss of family through divorce or rebellious children."

Because of these hypnotic expectations, it is easy for a pastor to barter the important for the immediate. Describing his frayed emotions, a veteran spiritual leader writes about the complicated demands he is experiencing: "Exhaustion comes to me from just thinking of the many more complex predicaments people bring to their pastors these days, let alone trying to help them with the problem." Like cancerous cells in the human body, these priorities and unrealistic expectations may multiply and feed on themselves.

Is this what God intended for ministry? The answer is a resounding no! Some clear thinkers consider all this agitation about expectation to be a contradiction of the faith we preach.

On this point, a thoughtful pastor from New England opens windows of grace for others while criticizing himself: "To a great extent I am victim of expectations, my own and others. Many of us who preach grace as a way of life do not practice it in relationship to our ministerial tasks. We are more eager to please the people than we are to rest in the fact that God wants to use us the way we are. We preach grace and practice a theology of works."

A serious attempt to reconcile grace with expectations and dependence with duty may provide the much-needed answers we seek. What liberating freedom comes to a pastor's mind when he realizes his best self and his noblest efforts are good enough for God.

## Discovering Solutions

Why not start a one-person campaign to reshape concepts of ministry among opinion shapers in your congregation? Include yourself in this revolutionary exercise. Too often a pastor considers existing expectations to be fixed and static and unmovable, but they can be changed. Since expectations are molded by so many people, it is possible to begin changing them bit-by-bit—among lay leaders, committees, individuals, and church members.

Think of the payoff of truly visionary expectations. You might consider the following strategies for reshaping expectations in the church you serve.

● *Develop "Expectmanagement" Skills*
"Expectmanagement" is as old as ministry itself. It simply means the ability to use expectations to create an exciting church and cultivate fulfillment for the pastor. In the process, the pastor gives benign neglect to unrealistic expectations.

A caution: pastors are sometimes so busy resisting unrealistic expectations that they become blinded to beneficial ones. As a corrective, focus on productive expectations and then respond positively to them.

"Expectmanagement" means a leader does not ignore all expectations as notions of impractical dreamers. Someone must respond to the heart cries of committed Christians who want their church to be better, to recognize an idea whose time has come, and to anticipate what may be needed tomorrow.

● *Define Ministry for Yourself*
A few pastors have such a foggy view of their work that they call everything ministry; playing ball with their children, mowing the lawn, or visiting a neighbor are worthy activities but not ministry. Other pastors feel confused by a collision of roles and division of labor between pastor and laypeople or between pastor and spouse. Some pastors have unclear concepts on the location of ministry, so they wonder if it is done

**63**

on the street or in the study. And others have a murky notion of time required to build a profession, so they are either involved every waking moment or handle time like a wealthy country gentleman with no schedule to keep and no place to go.

A sweeping gap of what constitutes effective ministry exists between lay and clergy perceptions. That is why a pastor must ultimately define and implement the meaning of ministry for himself in a congregation. To know what one is doing and why solves many questions, clarifies how ministry can be expected to affect individuals in the congregation, and provides a comfort zone for those who are threatened by ambiguity.

To define ministry does not mean it is arbitrarily determined only by the pastor's personal preferences, prejudices, or perspectives. Rather the conscientious minister's definition will be informed by Scripture, denominational understanding of the doctrine of the church, lay and clergy church leaders, theological training, and colleagues in ministry.

Having done all to grasp data from these sources, the pastor must then define ministry for himself, making sure it is acceptable to God and appropriately accountable to the church. In this process, the pastor always does himself a favor to recognize that the church is a voluntary organization where people vote approval or rejection with attendance and money.

The next step in defining ministry is for the pastor to clearly articulate his concepts of ministry to the governing decision group and the congregation, both individually and collectively.

Such a forthright discussion must make room for adjustment and input from laity because they have entrusted their spiritual development to the pastor. In the secular workplace, this dialogue is called negotiating. In the church it is a congregation-wide clarification of what ministry really is. The role of a pastor is best negotiated when the relationship is being formed.

All of these processes give laypeople a new understanding of what ministry should be and allows them an opportunity for valid input. They have a right and a need to be heard. Their concerns inform a pastor's understanding of the church, the community, and the world in which ministry is done. At the same time, this dialogue helps shape congregational views of ministry.

The main purpose for defining ministry is not to draw battle lines or cause conflict, but to provide in-depth communication that can strengthen the church, inspire the laity, and build vital relationships for the pastor. Through this dialogue-defining effort, the pastor and key lay leaders construct a strong foundation for wholesome future expectations by the whole people of God.

● *Evaluate Expectations by the Golden Rule*
Absurd expectations can be spotted quickly in others but are more difficult to detect in ourselves. While a pastor usually considers his expectations as visionary and right, he may view expectations by others as unreasonable or even preposterous.

This two-way process of creating and receiving expectations can be tricky. In our town last Sunday, a well-known pastor expounded utopian concepts for the congregation while openly scorning something another had expected of him. Too bad churches do not have umpires to call "foul ball."

Charity and grace are especially needed when the laity's only frame of reference for ministry is a universalizing of their own past experience. For example, a family from rural Ohio now living in metropolitan Miami expects their pastor to do his work the way their grandfather's pastor did fifty years ago in a rural setting. Ministry in such a different context simply cannot be done the way they remember it being done. Of course, their stubborn stand on methodology is regrettable, but the pastor's response should be effective ministry to all people, even those who do not appreciate his style. He cannot withhold ministry because of a disagreement about style.

● *Exhibit a Christ-Saturated Life*
Live and serve on such a high plane that you go well beyond your expected or legal obligations in marriage, finance, and

use of time. John Wesley said of early Methodists, "Our people die well." Why not give the church reason to say, "Our pastor lives well—better than anyone I have ever known. I want a similar quality of life."

Reasonable people notice when Jesus Christ is allowed to enrich details of the minister's life, and they come to a godly pastor's defense when others are overly critical about unmet expectations. In fact, those same supportive people may adopt the pastor's modeling as their pattern for Christ-quality living in a secular world.

● *Commit to Excellent Ministry*
A miraculous cure for unrealistic expectations is to provide distinguished ministry, especially in highly visible areas such as preaching, worship, or pastoral care. Word then gets around that the pastor does his work as well or better than any previous minister.

Such an excellent expression of ministry gives a pastor a credit line of credibility needed to weather tough times. It is a fact of ministry that many congregations overlook a pastor's faults when they know he serves competently in other important phases of ministry.

Realize all expectations cannot be met. Contrary to prevailing opinion, a pastor cannot be all things to all people. But availability during emergencies must be given high priority. Emergencies are not always the obvious: major illness, death, emotional crises. They may be "passages": death of parents outside the congregation (easy for a pastor to overlook), extended joblessness, or more ordinary illnesses. People who are served well in times of crises will be forgiving and gracious about unmet expectations. Get control of your time so you can maximize your achievements, then leave the rest to God.

● *Accept the Reality of Unfinished Work*
A pastor's work is never totally completed. That means some unfinished tasks hound him at the end of every day and wait for him the next morning.

The pressing question is what will be left undone, and what will be given priority tomorrow. Every demand does not have equal importance and urgency. Pastors must constantly struggle to prioritize ministry demands.

● *Focus on the Meaning of the Term "Pastor"*
Why are you a pastor? Many enjoy the title or position without embracing the tasks and relationships. For them, being a pastor is a professional attainment rather than a life-changing opportunity, a profession rather than a calling to serve Christ's church. Pastoral work always comes into clearer focus through a self-talk question, "What does the Father want me to do as pastor in this assignment today?" This focus brings ministry to life.

To cope fairly with expectations, pastors need an organizing center to give direction and focus to their work. This is a transforming insight. You must seek God's priority in each ministry situation as your centering focus. Above everything else, the pastor must deliberately care for the spiritual needs of people; their spiritual maturity is never automatic, nor does it come by osmosis.

● *Know the Difference between the Few and the Many*
Do not allow a minority to determine your perspective or set your ministry agenda. Always consider who said what—the word of a faithful saint carries more weight than a grumble from a recreational complainer. It is unfair and inaccurate for an entire congregation to be judged by the attitudes and actions of a few. Try not to confuse the whole with the part. One grousing member is not a reason to preach a fiery sermon or a cause to resign. The majority are usually fair-minded in their expectations. Trust the evaluation of the many over the judgment of the few.

Try not to overgeneralize about either the critic or the affirmer. The work of the church is shot through with the notion that one vocal person speaks for several or many. More often than not, they speak for themselves only and almost never for God. It is good to remind yourself that even difficult people have no pastor but you, so they need your acceptance and forbearance.

## THE CONTEMPORARY CHALLENGE
## FOLLOW THE FATHER'S AGENDA

Brothers on the way—the only appropriate pattern for determining the pace and priorities for ministry is to find and follow the Father's plan.

In far too many instances, confusing commotion dominates ministries because a pastor feels obligated to listen to so many voices and tries to please too many people. Everyone has his own opinion. The pastor hears conflicting expectations at home and chuch. Denominational leaders and ministerial peers add their advice. He even hears it at the corner convenience store from the sixteen-year-old clerk behind the counter. And a street beggar has his say, "Good preachers always give to people like me—you can't be much of a pastor."

All this confusion needs clarification. Even if a pastor were able to accomplish everything everyone wants done—an impossible assignment—he still might not please the Originator of his ministry. Since God inaugurated your call to Christian service, He must have something important in mind for you to achieve in your present setting. The ultimate issue is to discover what He wants by implementing the mandate of Scripture.

The dense fog caused by conflicting expectations starts lifting when a pastor leads the church into genuine spiritual achievement based on a biblical agenda. Then, entrenched murmurings about ministry may be reduced or stilled when new converts find Christ.

Use the Bible to establish the agenda for authentic ministry. Saturate your thinking with Scripture and then communicate the mission by every possible means. The Lord's ways lead to simplicity, achievement, and fulfillment. Pastor C.B. Hogue summarizes how Scripture shapes this process:

"Who sets my agenda? I do. But I base my decision on Scripture, God's Spirit, an informed, trusting relationship with the board, and knowledge of the church's needs, my abilities, and my motives."[2]

Faithfully activate the biblical mandate in your church. Then stop stewing about what all the novices and specialists say about methods and marketing and expectations and obligations and cultures and opinions and options. For 2,000 years, people have been magnetically drawn to Christ's mission for the church and the world. And they still are, even in your setting.

## RENEWAL STRATEGIES
## HOW TO SHAPE THEIR EXPECTATIONS

✔ *Define Ministry for Yourself*
✔ *Evaluate Expectations by the Golden Rule*
✔ *Exhibit a Christ-Saturated Life*
✔ *Commit to Excellent Ministry*
✔ *Accept the Reality of Unfinished Work*
✔ *Focus on the Meaning of the Term "Pastor"*
✔ *Know the Difference between the Few and the Many*

**FOUR**

# Warning:
# Ministry May be
# Hazardous to
# Your Marriage

"Thanks for not divorcing my mother."—a pastor's teenage son from Ohio

H er honest question deserved an honest answer.
"Why do I hear so much about pastors' marriages going bad? Even before we came to school, we had a great marriage that I rated a ten. Now I wonder if we will face unusual pressure next year." The questioner, a thirty-one-year-old mother of two and an expert computer programmer, married a plumber eight years ago, long before he thought about ministry.

Their family made an amazingly positive adjustment while the husband/father attended Bible college. However, as he finishes pastoral preparation, she is bothered about possible marriage pitfalls in the parish.

She continued, "My friend, whose husband has been a pastor for five years, contends every couple going into ministry should have two identical signs artfully lettered with the message, *Warning: Ministry May Be Hazardous to Your Mar-*

*riage*. One sign should be hung in the pastor's study about eye level with his desk and the other hung in their bedroom.

"She thought the office sign would remind her husband of potential problems in counseling and overwork, while the bedroom sign would remind both wife and husband that, without persistent determination, ministry competes for priority, sensitivities, and intimacies in marriage."

We responded to this future pastor's wife, "Most marriages of couples in ministry are strong and healthy. We just don't hear about them because good marriages do not make juicy gossip." That led to a long chat about how a pastor and his wife can give each other a satisfying marriage.

Ministry either strengthens or stresses marriage; it seems there is little middle ground. Difficulties drive some couples to blame normal problems on the ministry. Difficulties for others are turned into adventure, so they strive for an ideal relationship where both husband and wife are more fun to be with when they share a cause worth living for. A deliberate decision to build a strong marriage makes the difference. Then fragile marriages become solid, get-by marriages become special, and great marriages become grand.

## Things Have Changed in Pastors' Marriages

The women's revolution has left many pastors and wives confused and challenged about their marriages, often compelling them to renegotiate their relationships with each other and with the church. Fuller Seminary psychology professors Mickey and Ashmore accurately depict the way it used to be: "In

### RISK FACTORS

Marriage Problems Pastors Face:
- 81% Insufficient time together
- 71% Use of money
- 70% Income level
- 64% Communication difficulties
- 63% Congregational differences
- 57% Differences over use of leisure
- 53% Difficulty in raising children
- 46% Sexual problems
- 41% Pastor's anger toward spouse
- 35% Differences over ministry career
- 25% Differences over spouse's career

*Leadership,* Fall 1992

an earlier era of clergy marriages, we find unambiguous, stylized roles and behavioral expectations. The early portrait is of a family in which the minister is male, the spouse is a faithful Christian homemaker who reflects the virtues of the Virgin Mary, works with the spiritual industriousness of the mystics, and is willing to martyr herself on behalf of her pastor-husband and 'his' church."[1] Everyone can cite submissive examples and stormy exceptions.

Pastors' wives, in earlier times, often felt victimized as unpaid servants of the church: married to imperfect husbands whom others imagined to be carbon copies of the Lord. Sadly, the wife knew better about her human husband. Either willingly or grudgingly, she was cooperative or even subservient while at the same time being lonely, troubled, and often aloof.

Society, the church, and women have irrevocably changed, even though traditional thinking prevails in many minds and in some congregations. Consequently, expectations by all three have been altered and become vastly more complicated. New roles for men and women have unsettled long-held assumptions regarding marriage, parenting, and church connections. But out of this fierce societal debate can emerge a constructive opportunity to improve relationships rather than ruin them.

The issues, however, are much deeper than freedom from rigid expectations. Rather, genuine liberation to grow healthy marriages begins when a pastor and wife discover and nurture the quality relationship they wish to have with each other. A high-satisfaction marriage starts with a shared willingness to help the other be his or her best self. Such an exceptional marriage takes time, insight, sensitivity, priority, and mutuality.

Then too there is a church issue that needs dialogue and negotiation. Pastors and churches must be sensitized to the fact that the health of a pastor's marriage and the well-being of the church depend to a large degree on each other. A pastor with a problem marriage seldom does his work well. And a troubled church seldom ministers effectively to its pastor or his family. A weakness in one paralyzes the other.

Competition between marriage and ministry must cease. Every personal effort a pastor makes to strengthen his marriage is a gift he gives himself, his spouse, and the church. Those efforts also protect the couple from the moral midnights that surround them. Much more serious dialogue about these issues are needed on every level of church life.

## Pain in Pastoral Marriages

Incidents of emotional and legal divorce, separation, immorality, and loss of intimacy are exploding through the roof. Listen to the anguish that arrives almost daily in H.B.'s mail.

- *Temptation:* "In my marriage, almost daily I am tempted to succumb to the lust of the flesh, the lust of the eye, and the pride of life."

- A *statistic:* "I feel as if I am a statistic waiting to be counted, that at any time I might fall to immorality. These thoughts do not consume me, but they do gain my attention often."

- *Cycle of pain:* "I need help to get out of the biting, picking, and bickering cycle in my marriage. We do destructive things to each other."

- *Children suffer:* "One morning after her dad resigned the pastorate and moved in with another woman, my little girl was crying so hard that I told her to be strong; and she said, 'Mommy, my strong is broke.' "

- *Divorce:* "I have been a workaholic concerning ministry and it cost me my family. Recently my wife filed for and obtained a divorce, taking our children with her. My life is lonely and empty now."

- *No emotional support:* "In reality, congregations neither value nor affirm a pastor who seeks to be a faithful family person as well as a faithful pastor. I sometimes wonder if they know what we feel."

73

- *Guilty for family time:* "I wish some organization would speak to the issue of people who feel guilty when they enjoy the family, particularly those who are committed to Christian ministry. Can't I have both?"

- *No affirmation:* "I get sidetracked into thinking ministry takes priority over home caring because I don't get much affirmation from home like I do when I am ministering to people."

- *Needs love:* "The burden of a critical, fault-finding, lukewarm church is pulling our marriage down fast. Is it wrong to want to feel loved and valued by our church?"

- *World's system:* "We hear the world saying it is okay to bail out once the going gets rough, and it is tough to counteract that."

- *Greatest need:* "Our greatest need is communication, tolerance, and patience between my wife and me! I feel she is unsupportive of me. We lack time together because we have separate ministries plus a three-year-old, a one-year-old, and number three due in three months."

- *Fear:* "I feel a danger of the cooling of the love relationship between my wife and me. Then another fatal attraction could arise."

- *Emotional separation:* "Many clergy couples are married but separated in heart."

- *Waste:* "Oh God, we've both tried so hard and failed so grandly. How many people will this hurt and how many souls may not be won because of this adultery? It is such a waste and I can't bear it."

**Renewal Principles for Strong Clergy Marriages**
Gordon and Gail MacDonald are well-known Christian leaders and authors. In our interview, they offer principles any couple

in ministry can use to strengthen their marriage. There is help for all clergy marriages here: renewal for troubled marriages, prevention for healthy marriages, and advice for new marriages.

## Interview with Gordon and Gail MacDonald

**London/Wiseman:** Thanks for your willingness to share insights about brokenness and restored marriage relationships. Before we begin, let's catch up on your present assignment.

**Gordon:** For the last four years we have been serving a fine congregation in New York City, the place where I was born. [The MacDonalds are now back serving at Grace Chapel in Lexington, Massachusetts.]

**London/Wiseman:** Tell us about your ministry pilgrimage before New York.

**Gordon:** Gail and I have been sharing ministry as long as we have been sharing life together—thirty-two years now. We started in a little church 175 miles east of Denver. Our longest pastorate was fourteeen years in Lexington, Massachusetts, near Boston, where we raised our family and had many happy experiences of ministry.

**London/Wiseman:** Both of you have contributed so much to so many pastors and their wives, especially through your books. What is the favorite of all your books?

**Gail:** That's a tough question—a little like trying to decide the favorite among your children. *Ordering Your Private World* is special to me because it was such a surprise the way heaven has used it.

**Gordon:** I think my two favorites are *Christ Followers in the Real World* and the one that Gail and I recently finished, *Till the Heart Be Touched.*

## Is Intimacy Being Starved in Pastors' Marriages?

**London/Wiseman:** *Till the Heart Be Touched* discusses intimacy and relationships, doesn't it?

**Gordon:** Yes. We deal with the question, is intimacy actually being starved in a world that is saturated with sex.

**London/Wiseman:** How do you define intimacy?

**Gordon:** We define intimacy as a passionate connection between two people. Though it is most intense in a marital relationship, it is also involved in friendship in a broader sense. The whole book deals with components that make intimacy possible and satisfying.

**London/Wiseman:** We remember *Rebuilding Your Broken World* where you describe ways to mend a broken world. How does that idea relate to intimacy, especially in marriage?

**Gordon:** In many ways. It is no secret that *Rebuilding Your Broken World* was written out of a time in my life where I personally experienced total, humiliating failure.

**London/Wiseman:** What special lessons did you discover in that broken place?

**Gordon:** In that dark night of failure, I was forced to ask: Does God have grace enough to squeeze restoration out of the worst a person can do by choice?

I learned that people commit sin and make terrible mistakes by their own choices. But those choices are surrounded by environments or conditions we allow or accept. Then we make choices, do things, and hold attitudes that would not have been possible if we did not allow the environment or conditions to exist. So it is important to recognize, reject, and correct those troublesome environments where bad choices could be made.

**Gail:** It is also important to recognize that some [people] suffer a broken world because of the rippling effect of evil and not because of their own choices. And so they are needing to rebuild their broken world, just like I needed to rebuild our broken world, along with Gordon. We needed to do this in tandem because we loved each other. All of us are affected by evil that we did not cause that breaks our world.

**London/Wiseman**: Gail, did you and Gordon write this book together?

**Gail**: Yes, writing helped us work through tangible ways to rebuild. I think the writing was a sacred trust as well as therapeutic.

## Deceit Makes You a Sitting Duck
**London/Wiseman**: Gordon, you wrote a powerful sentence: "Evil must be named and sin must be hated."

**Gordon**: I believe that! In my judgment, all sin begins with self-deceit. We lie to ourselves or someone else lies to us. In that spiritual fog—a definite blurring of truth—we believe a lie to be truth. Many sinful acts in the Bible are prefaced by glaring deceit.

**London/Wiseman**: How does that affect ministry and a pastor's marriage?

**Gordon**: For the sake of a healthy marriage, every pastor and his wife need to realize there are many deceitful messages in the contemporary climate. In those settings, you can be tricked into believing the consequences of your choice will not be as bad as you once thought. Or "I'll get away with this." Or "Everybody's doing it." Or "Maybe God doesn't care about my being a bit slippery at this point."

The first thing every man or woman in leadership needs to realize is that the minute deceit is allowed to enter your life, you are a sitting duck for some sinful impulse.

**London/Wiseman**: Do you think Bible personalities had a broken world experience?

**Gordon**: Many did. The number of people who did not have some crushing, shaming experience is a short list compared to those who did.

## A Broken World Portrayed
**London/Wiseman**: Can we make a clear connection between brokenness in the Bible and a modern pastor's marriage?

**77**

**Gordon:** Let me be specific. By broken world, I mean anything that has a catastrophic result which threatens or destroys a marriage, a ministry, a relationship, or a lifestyle.

**London/Wiseman:** Is it not a grave miscalculation to become smug and think such a failure could never happen to me . . . that I'm exempt . . . that brokenness cannot touch my life, my marriage, my ministry?

**Gail:** It is important to recognize that relationships are among our greatest strengths. Gordon and I spent all these years working on relationships with each other, with our family, and with our Lord. Yet relationships can be destroyed in an unguarded moment of fatigue or disillusionment.

## Destructive Lifestyle—Above Criticism and Correction

**London/Wiseman:** In a conversation with Dr. Dobson on his radio program, you once mentioned three lifestyles that lead to choices that produce broken worlds. Do you think those apply to all pastors and their marriages?

**Gordon:** They apply especially to pastors. Let's see if I can name them. Number one is the leader who places himself above criticism so he will not take counsel from others. He will not listen to rebuke, beginning first with his spouse and then close friends and working colleagues. And this happens easily because if you head a church or religious organization, you are likely to be a strong-willed person. Since people follow those with strong opinions and convictions, the leader often wards off others who want to erode his will and plan. This strength in a leader, which is so necessary for a clear-focused ministry, becomes a terrible hindrance.

**London/Wiseman:** How does that cause a broken world?

**Gordon:** The downside of this strength is that you stop letting people get through to you. You start out with something admirable, but you end up in a trap with strong callouses on your soul and your mind. Then you refuse to hear when people try to talk to you about the state of your soul, your moral condition, or your toxic attitudes that are erosive to your spiritual condition.

**London/Wiseman:** I heard of a minister whose members and staff say, "He has no one to say 'no' to him."

**Gail:** That is sad and scary. No one can possibly know it all, and being head of an organization does not make the leader smarter or more spiritual than other team and family members. It is easy for a pastor to be fooled by his own propaganda because he is supposed to be right.

**Gordon:** Let me illustrate from my own experience how much real effort it takes to be able to listen to criticism or correction. You see, I have stood at the door of a sanctuary and had more than a hundred people tell me that my sermon was the greatest they had ever heard. Then you go home, and your spouse or children want to criticize some dimension of your life. It is hard to listen and much harder to believe what they say.

**London/Wiseman:** Then you believe your own press and wonder how those at home could possibly be right.

**Gail:** Yes, and you flow toward where you are going to get strokes rather than to reality or what might be helpful.

## Destructive Lifestyle—No Familiar Boundaries
**Gordon:** That is exactly right, and the second destructive lifestyle that encourages a broken world is what I call a traveling lifestyle.

**London/Wiseman:** How does that apply to a pastor whose ministry is mostly in the local setting?

**Gordon:** Let me explain. One of the greatest restraints to sin is a kind of fixed community like a neighborhood, village, small town, or even a church where people know you well. This is a place where you are committed to the norms and behavior patterns of this group of people day-by-day. I grew up in a community like that where the neighbors took the responsibility for rebuking or correcting you. So you were a pretty good kid under those constraints.

**London/Wiseman:** Now it becomes who cares or who will know? How do you see this being played out in contemporary pastoral ministry?

**Gordon:** I think we need to face a plain fact that about an inch beneath our Christian skins is a barbarian inside us who is desperately wanting to get out and express himself. The moment there are no restraints, even passive restraints, a person may be in a vulnerable condition – open to a destructive response to an alluring temptation. The problem comes from lack of obvious restraints more than miles traveled.

## Destructive Lifestyle – Addicted to Success
**London/Wiseman:** What is the third lifestyle that contributes to a broken world?

**Gordon:** It has to do with success in any dimension of life like money, prominence, power, or even marriage.

**Gail:** Successful people begin to feel indestructible, so they possess ministry rather than manage ministry for Christ. They become oversensated by life so they cannot center down, be still, get redirected, or gain perspective. Then everything seems larger than life, so they begin to run on natural energy instead of divine enablement. In error they reason, "I didn't pray and I didn't seem to need it."

**London/Wiseman:** That trap comes to all pastors regardless of the size of their church. They think what they are doing is the most important thing in the whole world. Since God gave them this dream, they think, "I must be great. I must be good if He trusted me with this."

**Gordon:** Let me push this idea in another dimension. Gail and I have been blessed on occasion by the generosity of friends who have done things for us we could never afford. Many pastors, even in much smaller churches, have a similar kind of relationship.

Recently, we were treated like a king and a queen. Both of us quickly realized that anything that lifts you out of the realities of an average human being impacts you so you feel special and pampered—a severe problem for a pastor.

You begin to think of yourself as untouchable by all those things that do other people in. You're convinced you're immune to failure and that nothing is ever going to go wrong. Wrong!

**London/Wiseman:** So you think you are even beyond moral breakdown?

**Gordon:** Yes. And that kind of feeling of success tends to drive you to a kind of addiction—not addiction to alcohol or drugs or sex, but addiction to excitement and activity.

**Gail:** Sensation, really!

**London/Wiseman:** Thanks for explaining those three dangerous lifestyles.

**Restoration: Start with Repentance**
**London/Wiseman:** Let's talk specifically about your restored broken world. God gave you a second chance. Now, out of your brokenness, God has enabled you to touch thousands of people with a message of restoration and healing. Many pastors' marriages need a healing like you have received. Would you describe the process God used to heal you?

**Gordon:** As a starting point, the biblical concept of repentance must be taken seriously. You must come to a moment when you realize that deep in the innermost depths of your person is a foul, stinking mess called evil that defies rational description and is waiting to ambush the mind and twist the truth.

**London/Wiseman:** Is repentance once for all?

**Gordon:** I think it must be continuous because you do not repent of just an act, but a condition. That is why every man and woman stand on level ground before the cross. It is not because some of us have done sin number nine and others

**81**

have done sin number two or three. It is a condition which is potentially destructive. And I mean viciously destructive. Every day with fresh brokenness, I have to go back to recognize that the same evil that betrayed me several years ago may betray me tomorrow in a different way.

Gail: In six years of observing my husband, this repentance lifestyle has been an ongoing process. It has made it possible for us to live by the grace and mercy of God and continually extend mercy to each other.

## Add Mercy to Repentance
London/Wiseman: Tell us more about how you make this connection between repentance and mercy in marriage.

Gail: Well, mercy from me toward Gordon was possible because I have seen him give mercy to me and to others over so many years. Mercy is an important part of ministry for us and also in our relationship with each other.

London/Wiseman: Repentance and mercy—what powerful sources for building strong relationships between pastor and spouse in these risky times.

Gordon: Gail had to give an enormous amount of mercy to me, but do not think that came easy. Both of us know what it is like to live with real pain; but in the painful process, there was a purifying, a presence, and a tenderness of God at work in our lives. Now our marriage literally abides in a constant flow of a grace and mercy that makes me love my wife in a way that I never loved her before.

London/Wiseman: That's well stated and demonstrates the application of the biblical ideal to real life. Thank you for opening your heart like that. Could we move now to your ideas about significant others who served as accountability partners or as grace givers for you?

Gordon: Certainly. Those persons are necessary because you cannot forgive yourself, you cannot give yourself grace, and you cannot restore yourself. That has to be a gift, first from God, and then from significant persons in your life. In my world it was Gail and the children.

Then it comes from men and women who surround you and serve as a spiritual splint so healing can come. I find the example of the splint from medicine illustrates the healing process that has to take place.

**Gail:** Regrettably, lots of people find it difficult to accept discipline. But discipline is necessary for healing to take place.

## Add Mercy to Accountability

**Gordon:** Gail is right. The first indication that you are with someone that doesn't understand the need for discipline is when they say, "I've failed terribly, but how soon can I get back?" Usually it's a moral issue which seems to be a pet sin of pastors.

Anyway, they say, "What can I do and how long do you think it will be before I can be preaching again?" When someone asks a question like that, you realize they are trying to skip over the steps of healing. They are not interested in getting their souls scoured and finding out what went wrong. They're much more interested in how quickly they can get on with business as usual.

You must have accountability people so you can put yourself in their hands and say to them, "You are calling the shots right now, and I am going to totally submit to you."

**London/Wiseman:** Somewhere in your writing you said, "Restoration was a result of people who cared."

**Gordon:** That's the way it is. It cannot be "I feel sorry for you; you're my friend, and what can we do to make you feel better."

One grace giver said, "A player is deeply wounded down on the field and we have to get him help so he can play again."

**Gail:** That means hard things you have to hear, to do, and directives you have to take. For example, I can remember

Gordon pouring over the Book of Romans as part of this discipline. He was making it a personal book because it was so important to let the Word of God be the basis of his healing—not something psychological.

## Evaluate and Renovate the Environment

London/Wiseman: Let's be sure we understand the process. It is repentance, mercy, accountability to grace givers, and what comes next?

Gordon: Next, I did a careful inventory of environmental issues that allowed deceit to take place. This has made us respectful of fatigue concerns. In Gail's book *Keep Climbing,* she has written about disillusionment, which we realized we had gone through. And there is also much to discover about your own temperament.

Gail: In exploring environmental issues, we realized we did not pray enough. There was too much work and not enough diversion. We even discovered from the life of Elijah that he was given a 200-mile walk after an awful period in his life. We found we needed more laughter and friendship. So we have worked over the last six years at maintaining a friendship network; it has been proactive on our part because it is easy to lose contact with friends.

London/Wiseman: Gordon, in your book *Rebuilding Your Broken World,* you wrote that God has put all the pieces for rebuilding in place and the process has been time-tested.

Gordon: It's fun to have these ideas repeated back to me. I really believe that. The Bible has an endless string of men and women who came out of terrible situations and were restored in the grace and power of God.

Gail: One powerful passage that deals with mending nets is Galatians 1 where the Apostle Paul instructs us to restore each other gently. Nets are mended so they can be used again in the future.

**London/Wiseman:** Help us make application to our reader's situation. Just to be blunt, the things you have been through could have destroyed your marriage and can destroy other marriages. Lots of pastors and their wives are trapped in brokenness that may not have to do with moral failure, but they really need help in putting things back together. What is their hope?

**Gordon:** Their hope, like ours, is the Gospel. If the Gospel cannot heal the worst situations when people are yielded, repentant, and open to the disciplining, restoring grace of God, then the Gospel is not worth much. But we know the Gospel is worth everything because it was provided for us by the death and resurrection of Christ.

But there is another issue. People can have all the intention in the world of seeking healing for brokenness, but they will never find it if the Christian community around them is not committed to healing. And that is one of the tragedies going on across the world today in places where men and women have failed—the Christian community does not have the will to offer healthy healing.

When the church commits itself to a restorative ministry, then men and women will stop acting in self-righteousness and start with the tenderness of Galatians 6:1 to be committed to getting every broken player back on the field again to serve in the kingdom. I think we will see a revival spirit break out as we begin to act like we believe restoration is possible and desirable.

**London/Wiseman:** Building an environment for restoration is something every pastor, especially those with sound, healthy marriages, can do. We are challenged by the possibility that everyone can be involved in restoration, either as a giver of grace or a receiver of grace.

**Gordon:** I believe that with all my heart.

**London/Wiseman:** Thanks, Gail and Gordon, for sharing the depth of your pain and your incredible restoration.

## Tackle Tough Obstacles

The MacDonald interview underscores the fact that startling shifts in society and pressures in the church over stress pastoral marriages. Regrettably, too many settle for too little sparkle, too much tradition, too little intimacy, and too much concern for their image.

For starters, what can we do to help ourselves take more initiative? It is time to make adjustments, large or small, so our marriages can enrich ministries and ministries can strengthen marriages.

To alleviate stresses common to all marriages, the pastor and his spouse should take advantage of marriage resources in their community. Solid assistance is increasingly available through community agencies, school districts, and units of government. Useful programs can be located even in out-of-the-way places and sponsored by a variety of groups. Additional marriage materials may be secured through Christian bookstores, libraries, audio/videocassettes, counseling services, and seminars. And support groups for every problem from loneliness to communication to sexual dysfunction are being formed at a rapid pace across North America.

However, in the unique dimensions of clergy marriages, the pastor and his spouse must cultivate awareness and develop coping skills to deal with unique difficulties that are built into the fabric of ministry. The goal is not to struggle at a minimal level of fulfillment, but to create a stable, satisfying marriage that energizes ministry.

What makes clergy matches different from other marriages? What points of tension need to be considered? And how can these differences be positively used to deepen relationship and intensify pleasure? Let's consider several significant stress points.

1. *Competitive Vows.* If you are married, think back to your wedding and contrast those commitments against the ones you made at your ordination. In a basic sense, ordination covenants and marriage vows are in competition because both commitments are exclusive and binding; neither allows much

room for the other. This conflict is delineated by Malony and Hunt, "We have seen many variations on the nature of the ordination vow and on the nature of the wedding vow. Nevertheless, at some level the ordained minister will encounter a fundamental conflict between the two."[2]

*2. Incessant Emotional Overload.* The pastor's work, seldom physical but always bearing spiritual overtones, frequently causes emotional roller coasters. Within the period of a day, he might rejoice with the parents of a new baby, visit an unwed mother and her grieving parents, and cry with a dying child— perhaps all in the same hospital. Or after rejoicing in the faith of new members in a morning worship service, he may be soothing and counseling a battered woman at a shelter that afternoon.

The pain, emotional struggles, and declining commitments of others, coupled with his own fatigue, discouragement, and despair, take a toll on a pastor's whole being and leave him with almost no reserve for his family or himself.

Then when he gets home, he often finds the emotional climate to be different than he expected. With all the demands he encounters, the pastor needs home to be a safe sanctuary where he can take his tired body and battered spirit to be recharged by the people he loves most. He often discovers a slight problem, however. Family members are not ready to have him dump his load on them. By the time he gets home, they may have had all the pressures they can handle for one day—Mom's work schedule, his son's rained-out baseball practice, a mailbox full of bills, a car problem, or his daughter's double homework assignment.

One pastor's wife said it better than any outsider could, "I've worried many times about my husband's overload. I am sorry as I can be, but I have to keep the children protected from church problems and try to get ready to do my own job tomorrow. I am ready for him to resign from this madness whenever he has had enough."

*3. An Out-of-Sync Schedule.* Contacts with people, a vital ministry component, must be done mostly on evenings and

**87**

weekends. And Sunday is the pastor's busiest day. How could these demands of ministry be more out of sync with the needs of his family and marriage? The times he needs to see other people are the exact times his family is available and needs him the most. In addition, he has personal needs to be with them.

Traditionally, ministry is blamed for the notion that a pastor is too busy for his family. The real issue, in fact, is out-of-sync schedules. The problem almost always deepens in dual-occupation families because of a spouse's fixed work schedule (plus commute time), and the pastor's evening and weekends obligations.

Pastors need to be creative in designing flexible time schedules. They must find ways to be available when their spouses and families are. This may mean moving ministry activities to other time slots. Begin with small improvements if you cannot make major alterations.

Specific shifts need to be made depending on the children's ages, school schedules and calendars, spouse's commitments, and church programs. In the process, church calendars need to be evaluated in terms of achievement versus activity — many busy churches do not accomplish as much as they think.

*4. Temptations Resulting from Endless Contacts.* Unlike physicians, counselors, or lawyers, a pastor sees parishioners in numerous settings as he serves them in many roles. In a short time frame the pastor may preach to them, counsel them, visit their homes, serve them communion, attend or participate in common athletic events, enjoy social contacts, and offer comfort in times of loss.

Some therapists who specialize in clergy cases believe this creates a situation where it is easy to develop intimate relationships, a process which is gullibly misunderstood by too many pastors.

The enticements that result from frequent contact may be especially tempting, for example, if a pastor is counseling a woman and knows her marriage problems. Malony and Hunt explain, "It is difficult to keep one's position clear while becoming involved in a variety of relationships with others. There is a decided tendency in such situations to lose perspective, to become grandiose, and to use faulty judgment."[3] Those three factors—lost perspective, grandiose ideas, and faulty judgment—spell potential trouble for any occupation, but especially in ministry.

5. *Diverse Patterns of Marriages.* Patterns of pastoral marriages also have unique intricacies and distinctive time and intimacy demands. It should be noted that some marriages will take elements from more than one of the following models:

• *Partners in ministry* is the conventional pattern where the wife stays home and shares with her husband in as many details of ministry as possible. By definition, this relationship encourages immeasurable interdependency, so the pastor's decision-making is greatly influenced by his wife's outlook. The wife in this marriage model makes calls, leads Bible studies, and has high visibility in ministry to women. The flaw is that both partners are sometimes so influenced by the other's viewpoints that an accurate reality test is not possible. They begin to think alike, and some people say they begin to look alike.

• *Ministry is his business* is an independent relationship where the pastor does his ministry as a profession and the wife is largely uninvolved in the work of the church. In this pattern, the wife participates in church life at about the same level as an average layperson. Often the pastor explains this pattern by saying, "My wife's ministry is keeping me together."

• *The wife brings home the bacon* is a pattern where a valiant woman works outside her home because of economic necessity. She may even carry most of the family financial burden on her shoulders. Sometimes her salary keeps church doors open; without her job, there would be no church to attend and no pastor to lead. These women are among God's unsung heroines; however, this pattern often produces weary isolation, unresolved hostility, and lack of confidence in the husband's ability to earn a living.

• *The two-career pattern* is very familiar on the secular economic landscape and is often chosen by clergy couples. As we noted earlier, this arrangement may mean that the wife's career sometimes takes priority over her husband's ministry. She may make more money than her husband, and the possibility of a job transfer may complicate the relationship. This model makes it difficult for the pastor to consider a new assignment and can cause dissension if he is called upon to resign to follow his wife in her career.

## How to Nurture a Beautiful Pastoral Marriage

As we have seen, cultivating a satisfying marriage is an important part of emotional and spiritual wholeness. A commitment to marriage development provides a significant way to live a quality life that is pleasing to God, fulfilling to both partners, and healthy for the church.

In a conversation about adventures he desires from his marriage, a pastor remarked, "Since we plan to be married for a lifetime, we think it's worth earnest effort to make it all it can be—at least as much effort as getting a good education." He is right.

Marriage offers joy, meaning, and pleasure. The intense, demanding dimensions of ministry, that many consider harmful to marriage, can be used to cultivate closeness that grows out of sharing thoughts and experiencing service together. One pastor's wife caught the idea, "The more we discuss and the more we do in ministry, the more we discover we want to do and to talk about. Being married to someone who is not a minister must be a pretty dull life."

What follows is a partial "to do" list that is intended to help you maximize the potential in your marriage.

• *Allow Marriage to Add Adventure to Ministry*
A satisfying marriage is near the top of all life's joys. It is a sad misconception to think ministry and marriage are in com-

petition when they can complement each other so well.

Every generation has discovered that a good marriage makes all else in life better, while a poor marriage somehow diminishes it. Though separation or divorce in his own marriage creates immense image complications for a parish pastor, the larger problem is the emptiness that comes from the loss and the gloom in his inner world of what might have been. Every pastor's marriage can be improved by renewed commitments. The challenge is to establish a healthy relationship with the church that allows you to maintain an independent life as a couple and still maintain a loving, available, and guilt-free connection with the congregation. Only you can set the limits and enjoy the adventure.

● *Focus on Process*

Much happiness in a good marriage results from the process of spending years together, in good times and in bad. Many suggestions in the MacDonald interview lend themselves to continual process and intentional improvement.

Like all good marriages, a pastor's marriage is made up of covenants and celebrations—the first date, the proposal, the wedding, the vows, the reception, the honeymoon night, the birth of a child, and growing old together. But marriage is also made up of moments when gratitude is given, misunderstandings are healed, sick children are nursed to health, and customary rituals are observed. A fulfilling marriage is much more than a state or condition; it is actually a series of moments and events connected by commitments to each other and tightly linked to the grace of God.

● *Spot Warning Signals*

Too many pastors and their spouses believe the work of ministry and the financial support of a congregation have them locked into their present ways of relating to their environment and to each other. Though it takes deliberate effort, why not rethink any issue in your marriage which presents difficulty or dissatisfaction before you are forced to do so, or worse yet, before you settle for a dreary, non-fulfilling relationship.

● *Live by Spiritual Principles*
Practice grace, forgiveness, and mercy in the details of your marriage. To onlookers, there is something powerfully magnetic about a marriage that puts biblical principles into practice for all to see. Such a healthy, wholesome marriage shocks secular people with its durability and quality.

But there is much more. Marriage vows energized by love offer you a gratifying way to live. Christ the enabler helps us create a high standard of communication, friendship, and intimacy that others seek to imitate. Pastors and their wives may teach more about healthy marriage by how they live than by all they preach and teach.

● *Commit to Wholeness*
To enjoy a high-octane marriage, two pressing inner issues need constant tending by the pastor and his wife: spiritual reality and emotional nourishment. Effective ministry cannot be done by either partner without these elements in abundant supply. Whatever the cost in money, time, or priority, constant emotional and spiritual care must be given to make marriages stronger. Create a caring environment where you both nourish spiritual reality and emotional strength in the other. Cherish the fact that you have someone at your side through the thick and thin of ministry who loves you and cares about your well-being more than anyone else on the earth. Then you will have each other long after the current crisis is past.

● *Put Marriage on the Calendar*
Pastors are generally faithful to whatever they write in their datebooks and calendars. Why not put your wife into your datebook one night each week? When asked for some of your time that night, you simply respond, "I'm sorry, I have a prior commitment. Could we get together at another time?"

Guard that date night with tenacity; let nothing get in the way of that private time.

To enrich a happy marriage investment, the pastor and his wife should plan one evening a week together. Couples can bear most burdens together if they have a set time to discuss or resolve troublesome issues.

● *Rekindle Love*
In every possible way, continually rekindle your love for your mate. An old love reawakened can be more fun and a thousand times less destructive than a new one. It also has God's approval and will be satisfying to you and a source of reassurance to your mate—what a combination! Chaplain and veteran pastor Richard C. Halverson is right, "Every struggle we have that could be used as an excuse to separate or divorce is the very material God wants to use to create intimacy in our marriage."[4]

## THE CONTEMPORARY CHALLENGE
### MAKE YOUR MARRIAGE STABLE AND SATISFYING

The common thread throughout this chapter is that every marriage can be better and that happily married pastors are more effective pastors. Pastors unite, the time has come to stand up and get serious about our own marriages.

Haven't we seen enough marriage heartache and brokenness in those we serve? Haven't we observed the horrible results of infidelity in ministry, leading only to perpetual disappointment and misery? And though we are fully committed to healing and grace giving, can't we see that prevention in our own marriages is 10,000 times better than the most gracious, wholehearted restoration?

Let's pay the full price to make our marriages solid, satisfying, and spiritually sound. Let's move up on our list of priorities our commitments to emotional, spiritual, and physical intimacy. It's time in our own marriages to demonstrate all we preach to others about commitment, integrity, accountability, and virtue.

Let's do it because it is right and fun. Let's do it to make the Father rejoice. And let's do it to provide a model of a Christ-centered marriage for those who follow us.

---

### RENEWAL STRATEGIES
### HOW TO HAVE A HIGH OCTANE MARRIAGE

✔ *Allow Marriage to Add Adventure to Ministry*
✔ *Focus on Process*
✔ *Spot Warning Signals*
✔ *Live by Spiritual Principles*
✔ *Commit to Wholeness*
✔ *Put Marriage on the Calendar*
✔ *Rekindle Love*

---

# FIVE

# Showcase Kids or Stable Families?

"It has become a juggling act. We fight for every minute of quality time at home. We have set aside time as ours and it has become hallowed." — a pastor from Washington

T here is little more embarrassing to a pastor than the crises brought on by his wayward children. A disruptive family can wreck a pastor's reputation. If he can't control his own children, how can he manage the flock of God?

To face these issues, we're going to take a close look at such a situation. Consider the following true scenario; the names have been changed to protect the *innocent* and the *guilty!*

Ted Abbott, a pastor highly respected by young ministers, lives down the road in the next town and sounds like somebody everybody knows.

Abbott, age forty-five, grew Old First Church from 225 to 400 members in four years. He is proud of his achievements and boasts of tripling attendance in two previous churches. Honored by his denomination last year as pastor of the year, Ted has reason to be assured and he shows it.

Ted and Pat married twenty-five years ago while they were students in a Christian college. Both rate their marriage nine on a scale of one to ten. Pat, a gifted second-grade teacher, considers herself a career professional. The Abbotts have three children: Josh, sixteen; Tim, fourteen; and Sally, eleven. Most of the time, the family seems supportive of Ted's ministry. Church members enjoy bragging about their minister's family.

Recently, Josh generated a family earthquake when he was dismissed from school for drinking on the high school campus. Two fellow students accused Josh of supplying them with alcohol during lunch break. The town is full of talk, and Pastor Ted is especially embarrassed among lay church leaders.

Though Pat feels humiliated, she is consumed with closing a school year and renewing her state teaching credentials. Being a mother, wife, "holy woman" in residence, and teacher keeps her plate too full. Deep down she thinks Josh was experimenting, but blames Ted's emotional and physical absence from the family as the root of the problem. The other children are affected too; Tim is bewildered and Sally cannot quit talking about the situation.

Few outside the family know the private Ted who is proud and high strung. He worries that Josh's actions will tarnish his ministry. Ted is committed to controlling the church at any cost because he enjoys pyramiding every kind of power. For years, Ted Abbott has been pampered by family and church, so he thinks of himself as something special. His inner spiritual resources are dry and brittle.

Josh doubts his father's sincerity about ministry. Some family friends think Josh is unconsciously acting out resentment toward his father.

Ted believes Pat's professional teaching commitment is the real problem. He blames the church for not being more affirming of his family. It is his pattern: blame is more important than solving a problem.

This incident forces Pastor Abbott to evaluate relationships to his son, to his other children, and to his church. While hiding his true feelings from Josh, Ted strains to deal with his outrage and chagrin. He really wants the best for his family, but he wonders how he can face the congregation Sunday.

His feelings are complicated even more by a wise old church member who reminds him, "You only have two years left before Josh leaves home for college. Make the most of it for his sake."

How can Abbott deal with the crisis? As a pastor, he has sterling success, but he feels like a failure as a parent.

## Family Growth in Motion
Because of the crisis the Abbotts—Ted, Pat, Josh, Tim, and Sally—have a rare opportunity to grow together with increased acceptance, forgiveness, and insight. If used for family growth, the natural embarrassment is a small price for the benefits everyone can receive, especially Josh. Above all else, the children must know they are not on display for the sake of their father's ministry.

### A Mirror to Check Values in the Family
It is a given of family life that parents, regardless of their line of work, must endure some impulsive behavior by their children.

But what is going on inside Josh must be given top priority in this circumstance. As a part of the solution, Ted and Pat must come to terms with blaming each other. In the process, two important principles apply: (1) kids are more important than reputations, and (2) doing right produces good impressions rather than good impressions producing right. Thus, unconditional love will help carry Josh to adulthood and teach his pastor-dad several life-changing lessons.

### Parenting Adult Children
The elderly layman was right when he pushed Pastor Abbott to face the fact that Josh would soon be leaving home for college, a colossal step on the road to adulthood. The reminder about limited time was absolutely correct.

But the helpful friend completely missed the possibilities of a coming adult relationship. This new phase, which parents

**97**

often miss, was about to start for the Abbotts. As long as they live, Josh and Ted can profoundly influence each other's faith, if they will. Parenting adult children works like that.

For all ministers, the crystal-clear message is get serious now about spiritual influence on your children. Get on with it; time is limited. This caution applies regardless of a child's age.

*Lay Support: An Unused Resource*
In every ministry setting, there are some nonjudgmental parishioners who have heartfelt interest in the pastor's children. Their concern grows from the same root as all compassion and grace—Christ Himself. Pastors often overlook their serious desire to help. A group of lay leaders recently reminded their pastor, "We know how to love confused teenagers because we have so many of our own."

The minority that mistreat pastors' families have been given too much publicity. Horror stories abound; many are true. But those reports need clarification because it is generally only one or two church members that hurt clergy families and not an entire congregation. A formal poll would reveal that most church members are patient and tender with preachers' kids. The problem of this silent majority is that they do not speak up often enough.

This universal lesson from Ted's experience teaches ministers that someone in the church has an enlightening word about family for the pastor when he is willing to hear. And many will walk through any fire with their pastor's family.

*A Bump in the Road*
Unacceptable conduct in a pastor's children should be viewed as a warning of things that could come. Every alcoholic starts with a first drink; thieves begin by stealing petty items.

But every undesirable act does not create a negative domino effect on one's entire future. Josh's conduct has to be confronted, to be sure; and Ted must satisfy himself about what the incident means to Josh and the family. Wise discernment is needed.

Ministers' children are often painted into a corner by one mistake and cannot figure out how to come back. Such distrust at home or church can encourage the youth to do the same thing again. Their immature reasoning says, "If you think I am bad, I guess I am, so I will keep showing you how bad I am." Such a downward spiral destroys relationships and faith — a result no one wants.

To bring Josh through, large doses of confession, forgiveness, and grace are needed in the Abbott home and at Old First Church. This is a perfect opportunity for family and church to demonstrate what they believe and to welcome an offender home as if he had never been away.

A wise doctor underscored this idea one night while treating an asthmatic child in a hospital emergency room: "This is a serious bump in the road, but not a life-threatening episode."

## Sincerity about Ministry

Josh questioned his father's sincerity concerning ministry. Though a child's suspicions may be inaccurate, parents need to evaluate every time a child hints at a question about their authenticity. The head man at home or church can easily fool himself without frequent reality tests.

At such a time, this self-diagnostic question may be helpful: "What am I doing that makes my children question my commitments to ministry?" Teens and children have uncanny ability to spot a phony. This does not mean a parent caves in to a pouting child's remark: "I do not think you are much of a minister." Such a word uttered in a fit of anger is probably not reliable.

On the contrary, every challenge concerning authenticity should be scrutinized against reality. Rejoice if you earn a 100 percent grade. If the results prove embarrassing, improve and retake the test.

What children observe in parents is what they eventually see in the Heavenly Father. A child's doctrine of God starts to form in the cradle as he or she interacts with parents.

**99**

## Clergy Couples Write about Positive Parenting

A good family requires more than money in the bank, an acceptable neighborhood, or top-notch schools. Unconditional love is the basic ingredient for successful family life. This love must be intentionally built into relationships. The primary hindrances to a healthy family are not environmental disadvantages, but rather the absence of lived-out love by the clergy couple for each other and for their children.

**RISK FACTORS**

Life for a pastor's family is not easy. In a recent *Leadership* survey, 28% of pastors who responded said being in the ministry was a "hazard" to family life, 16% said it didn't affect family life either way, and 57% thought it was beneficial. Whether they felt positive or negative about it, the vast majority (94%) admitted that those in the ministry are under pressure to have "an ideal family."

*Current Thoughts & Trends,*
December 1992

Heart-wrenching letters from clergy couples repeat a recurring theme—they consider it tough for children to grow up under the gaze of church members. To them, many parenting problems seem to revolve around their fishbowl visibility in the church and community. Some letters suggest these issues might be solved by involving children as part of the ministry team. Others idealize the life of the laity, thinking clergy families would avoid routine parenting frustrations if they were not in the ministry. Consider the serious concerns and lofty aspirations clergy couples write about their families.

*Uprooted Family and Church Politics—God Uses Ambiguities*
A pastor's wife in the Northwest writes: "We serve a mission congregation that is five years old. In the last three years, things have become extremely political and those who were the founding roots of this congregation have turned against us saying the church is not growing fast enough. Our bishop, the closest thing we have to a pastor, took their side and listened to the political garbage.

"Through the process my husband, Gus, was voted out of the church. Now our family will be uprooted from this lovely

100

area and good schools simply because of politics in the church.

"Our family has been living in limbo for six months. We have no place to go. I have been 'counseling' four sad children, not knowing what to tell them except, 'Life is not fair, but God is good.' To a teenager, those are hard words. It's difficult to explain to them that their dad has been diligently preaching God's Word, saving souls, and then a few families have the right to tell us to leave. I am trying not to lose heart."

*"Political garbage."* Church politics can be a messy reality wherever two or more are gathered together. Too often church relationships sour because a group tries to run kingdom work according to human wisdom and secular values.

Politics in the church may be a two-edged sword, leaving no one blameless or deserving the whole blame. Though issues may be one-sided or prejudiced, most problems grow out of poor decisions made by several people who fail to consider the possible fallout. Whatever the roots, the pain of trying to explain "no place to go" to a minister's family is unbearable.

*"Living in limbo."* Now Gus's family is forced to pay a high price for the group's decision. The children are shaken because they want to believe in God and their parents, and before this tragic misunderstanding they believed in the bishop and church leaders. Now they are confused. Forced waiting for the new assignment makes matters worse.

Even though the parents do not feel able to give it, these children need ministry. Parents must find grace to be strong for their children's sake. Reaching for remedies together as a family may be a productive healing process; perhaps each family member will be able to give a small part of healing to all. As a first step toward wholeness, this family must view their situation as a severe loss, akin to a death or divorce.

*"It's difficult to explain to four sad children."* Satisfying explanations for radical losses are always difficult to find. However, the spiritual health of the children in this family is the most important long-term issue, even more consequential

**101**

than another assignment. They must be protected from the heavy burden of losing trust in the church and all her people.

Parental confidence in God will eventually bind up the family's wounds, even though they are locked in a waiting mode. God often surprises us by turning what others intended for our harm to our good. Old Testament Joseph is a shining example (Gen. 50:20).

New assignments are God's specialty. Like a trapeze artist, this family must "let go" before they can move on to the next stage of life together. An insightful devotional writer calls this "the grace of relinquishment." But our fear of the unknown makes it difficult to let go.

Any family in ministry may be transplanted from a place, but they will never be uprooted from God's generous provisions.

*God Remembers Sacrifice—Or Is It Mere Inconvenience?*
A minister's wife in New York writes: "We serve an aging congregation in an inner city and minister to a welfare community. On Sundays my three kids are often the only ones in their Sunday School class. It's tough, but I try to communicate to them that God sees and remembers their sacrifices. After four years in this place, we pray for good Christian friends for our children, for a larger home (ours is 800 square feet), and for at least one or two solid leaders in our church."

*"The only ones."* This wife/mother carries a heavy load. She comforts herself and the children by reminding them that God sees and remembers their sacrifices.

She is wise to bring her children into the commitment circle of ministry so they will not feel deprived. Deliberate attempts should be made to help the children find friends: putting them in touch with young people in a nearby church, putting them in contact with students in a Christian school, or helping them get acquainted with another minister's family. This friendship cultivation which would happen almost automatically in a larger church must be intentionally fostered here.

*"Eight hundred square feet."* Space for living is a common problem among urban dwellers. This frustration might be lessened for this family by imaginative use of existing room; making family use of the church facilities; and exploring available public spaces, like libraries, museums, and parks. In one situation where a family lives near the building, they use the church's fellowship hall as their family room and do all church-related hospitality there. Another family uses the church as their study hall two nights each week; the children study their school lessons, Dad studies for his sermons, and Mom studies for her adult education class.

Creative ways of dealing with the space problem must be devised so the size of the home does not become the deciding factor about whether or not to continue ministry in this place.

*"God sees and remembers their sacrifices."* Sacrifice is a tricky word that should be used with extreme caution. Shades of meaning of the word easily change depending on circumstance and viewpoint. One's sacrifice is another's blessing. For example, the missionary who leaves family, receives low wages, and is required to adjust to new cultures. People at home speak of the missionary's sacrifice while the missionary talks of her privilege. Which is it?

Though ministry places some restrictive constraints on families, it also offers benefits not available to other children. These privileges may include tighter family bonds, opportunities to meet special visitors coming to the church, an extended family among the people of God, flexible time commitments by parents, and more service opportunities for Christ. Underscoring these possibilities helps children balance sacrifices against serendipities.

Kids are sturdy and durable people who can willingly endure a lot if they see the cause as worthwhile. One clergy couple tells their children every day, "You are privileged to be a pastor's kid."

*A Family in Christian Leadership — Allow Children to Help*
A minister from Montana writes: "Many pastors work so hard helping other people's families that they neglect their own.

My district leader asked me how I would resolve the conflict between ministry and family. My answer was to involve my family in ministry."

From a minister in the Northeast: "As a family involved in Christian leadership, we feel we must live our lives beyond reproach. How much involvement is good for the child and the family?"

*"Involve my family in the ministry."* Taking family into ministry is mentioned many times in letters from pastors. Some view it as a problem and others as a potential. An amazing surprise awaits most believers—the one who gives is often blessed as much or more as the one who receives.

Two extremes should be avoided in family ministry. The first is intensity. Ideally, a child's level of participation should be determined by his/her own growth potential, rather than the pressing survival needs of the church. The good of the child must have higher priority than the requirements of the church.

The second extreme is no involvement. For some ministers' families, the church is viewed as nothing more than Dad's place of employment. Such a perspective creates problems. Regardless of age or family ties, every Christian misses out if they do not have a church home where they serve and are held accountable for personal spiritual growth.

*"Good for the . . . family."* Few people, including pastors' kids, cherish the church if they do not give loving service through its ministries. And ministers' families feel less isolated from their pastor-father when they observe his work close up.

Family-operated farms of bygone generations offer an example: home bonds grew strong when family members worked side-by-side to harvest the crop and build up the farm. The same dynamics work in the church. As a result, a pastor's family can hang together in circumstances that might shatter their secular counterparts.

For ministers' families who live long distances from extended families, it may be helpful to allow the church to become a surrogate extended family. They will probably not do it unless you welcome them into your home *and* heart.

*"Beyond reproach."* Like all believers, the minister's family must live according to biblical standards and the model of Christ. The quality life that results will be a joy to the individual and pleasing to Christ; it will cut down on a thousand efforts to "second guess" what others think or say. What is pleasing to Christ will please every serious follower of the Lord Jesus, and the rest probably can't be satisfied anyway!

*Bad Kids from Good Homes — Trust Them to God*
A clergy spouse in the West writes: "Unfortunately 'bad kids' sometimes come from good homes. This bothers me because some of the elders in our church feel the pastor should step down if the children are not believers or are disobedient. Is it fair to have a man's whole pastoral career jeopardized because his children have fallen away?"

*"Is it fair?"* No, but God gave choice to human beings. Pastors' kids, like everyone else, can choose their own way, and they do. Thus children can go bad from any kind of home, and they can also go good. No guarantees are offered with parenting. When asked about raising children, one veteran summarized, "Do your best and trust God with the rest."

During the children's brief years at home, train them, love them, lead them, believe in them, and get them ready to let go. Every conscientious parent has a strong factor on his side — children never escape the shaping influence of a good home, whether it be housed in a mansion or a small apartment.

Long-term, a minister's effectiveness is not determined by his children's choices, good or bad. One of the most powerful witnesses a pastor can have to his family or surrounding society is to make a full-fledged commitment to modeling the biblical concepts of morality, fidelity, and faith in his home. In this pressure-cooker world, the strength and impact of a stable Christian family unit are as strong as ever. A trustworthy model of family togetherness in the minister's home helps halt the erosion of abiding values in our society.

*Cherish the Wonder Years—Busyness Does Not Last Forever*
A pastor's wife near Indianapolis writes: "Please excuse me for not taking out my typewriter for this letter. I have a five-year-old boy, a three-year-old girl, and an eight-month-old girl. I am sure they would all want to help me type, and I would never get this letter finished. As a bookkeeper and part-time baker, if I wait to recopy this letter, you may not get it."

*"They would all want to help."* Those precious first five years of a child's life should be cherished as a special gift from God. Sometimes when loads get heavy and days seem long, a parent of young children wonders if they will ever grow up. The answer is "yes" and very soon. Treasure those early years and know that the frustrations are worth it. Make the most of your molding influence on the children at the same time you enjoy the incredible richness they bring into your life. Bonding during the preschool years greatly influences a successful future for everyone in the family.

*Build Family into Your Schedule—*
*Be Present When You Are Present*
A pastor from South Carolina writes: "Yesterday my four-year-old daughter said, 'Daddy, don't you love us anymore? You didn't eat with us once this week.' I tried to explain, but my words didn't make much sense. I wonder if it is the meals I miss or something else she needs that I have failed to give her."

*"Daddy, don't you love us anymore?"* On the surface, the question sounds frightening. Thus, the father may paint a self-portrait of being a bad parent if he dwells on the long-term implications of her question. But he is not a bad parent. On the contrary, his concerns show he is probably an above average or good parent.

At four years old, the daughter likely means she needs him and wishes he were home more often. In place of giving a long explanation that she will not understand, this pastor can correct her lonely feelings by building more family time into his datebook, especially at mealtime. The idea is to spend energy correcting the issue rather than worrying about long-term consequences. Action is usually more useful than worry in parenting problems.

*"I wonder if it is something else she needs."* Highly motivated, task-oriented career people are often blind to the "present but absent syndrome." Here's how it happens. A tired pastor comes home for dinner after a long day of counseling, sermon preparation, and administrative duties. When he sits down to eat with his family, his mind can easily dwell on the details of the day rather than on the relationships that need cultivating around the supper table.

The first step for improvement is to recognize the problem. A few quiet moments to refocus after getting home can solve this difficulty. Listening to our children often provides a gauge on how well we are doing at being really present.

## How to Strengthen Stability in Your Home
Strengthening clergy families requires an intentional dedication to abiding "family values." Three assumptions are true:
(1) whatever the minister's family has is contagious in the church, good or bad;
(2) families should be viewed as a bundle of potential, satisfaction, and commitment; and
(3) habit is the main enemy of family renewal.

Begin strengthening family stability by searching for ways to enrich your home and family. Ideas for enriching families are available everywhere: in bookstores, libraries, and magazine stands. Many general recommendations for families will also work well for clergy families. Start doing what family leaders suggest and your heart sanctions. Changes need not be complicated, but they are essential because business as usual will not work in these troubled times. Start with simple basics; often a small adjustment makes a vast improvement.

Put into practice what you already know. You will be amazed at how satisfaction from your family increases as you start seeing them through eyes of enjoyment and potential. Fully accept and celebrate the fact that your lives are inter-twined forever—that is a long time.

Living in a minister's home, done well, allows a quality life you and your family might not enjoy in any other profession. Fine-tune family relationships to take emotional, spiritual, and physical development of each individual into account. Family religion can be fulfilling with toddlers and young adults, and every age in between.

● *Please the People Who Matter Most*
View your family not as a textbook example to be analyzed, but as a living segment of society headed by you, different from any other family in the world. Celebrate their uniqueness.

Look at your family relationships through the eyes of your spouse and children. Magnificent strengthening experiences can flow from what your children need and discuss. Ask them to talk to you about family, make their suggestions work, and give them credit. Simple words like "My children taught me to love" or "My family plans the most exciting vacations" are powerful affirmations that nourish affection. In fact, children are some-times more perceptive about family needs than their parents.

The finest, most imaginative ideas for togetherness and ac-tivities never go far if they are not owned by your family. Family stability never grows out of "I-told-you-to-do-it" talk.

● *Get Your Family in Tune with God*
Pastors tend to talk like preachers, act like preachers, and relate to their families like preachers. Drop your ministerial voice and religious explanations for a while so you can lead your family in discovery of meaning in Bible reading, prayer, praise, and compassion for needy people. Allow your children to see you as a human being who is hungry for God—some-thing significantly different than being a religious profession-

al. Ask your family to help you get to know God better. Expect pleasant surprises.

● *Feed Faith to Children*
Children are continually bombarded by pessimistic input about life, the church, and the world. They overhear much from their parents at home, friends at church, and neighbors in the community. Then too contemporary living fuels hopelessness midst all the news and ideas transmitted via the secular media.

They need an antidote to such an overdose. Feed children faith to stabilize their spiritual growth. Offer explicit examples of how God is at work in the church. Remind them of miracles you have experienced in your family. Talk to them about amazing victories in the Bible. Create an environment of faith.

● *Refuse to Blame Problems on the Ministry*
Without question, ministry has difficulties not common to other professions. But all problems in a pastor's life and home do not come from commitment to ministry. To blame consequences resulting from bad judgments on the ministry is to mislead children. To attribute the results of poor work habits to the church is an amazing and amusing myth. To explain away the leaking roof as God's will is to miss the lesson that neglected roofs often leak, both at the minister's as well as the layperson's home.

● *View Family As a Gift from God*
Few things in the human pilgrimage bring more joy than a stable family. As a special gift from God, you must invest in your family. The more effort you devote, the more the family repays in satisfactions. Family fulfillment even crosses generations. Open your heart to the rich possibilities built into your family connections. Nothing else, short of the grace of God, can gratify a pastor for as many years.

Ask God for a vision of what your family can be and how He wants you to fulfill that dream. A family in ministry is a

**109**

laboratory for living where love is the supreme ingredient. Amazing but true, family is a splendid miniature of what God wants His church to be.

● *Focus on the Present*
Years of schooling can condition clergy to dream of bright tomorrows after they finish coursework and become active as ministers. Sometimes this future focus lasts for a lifetime. As a result, some pastors spend their lives dreaming about what their next assignment will be, how many members they will have in the next place, and what they will attain someday. The trouble is that someday never comes; no one can be fulfilled by fluffy fantasies.

Equally damaging are rearview-mirror perspectives that control some ministers. They remember a past that never was and long to go back to old days which were more miserable than today. But a startling reality must be faced: the past is gone forever; all we have is today.

This present focus also needs to become specific in family relationships. When a minister goes home in the afternoon, he should leave problems in the car, concerns at the church, and the future in God's hands. Children need undivided attention. Today is tomorrow's happy memory, and it is the only time we have to build a stable family.

● *Start a Family Support Group*
Why not start a self-help parenting group for ministers? In the United States alone, there are more than 500,000 self-help groups organized around every imaginable concern. Think of the advantages for clergy families. Each self-help group supplies face-to-face interaction between persons who share experiences, feelings, and struggles. As a result, group members discover ways to make personal changes, mobilize support for a cause, strengthen each other, and get personally involved in each other's lives. A sense of comradeship develops between participants.

All these advantages are needed by ministers and their families. For example, the Abbotts had no experience in dealing with their first child's eagerness to be an adult; a group to discuss such matters would have helped immeasurably. The family living in small quarters in an urban setting could receive insight from discussing its frustrations with others in similar situations. And the mother who struggled with her three preschool-age children might get help from other women who have successfully survived similar situations.

To receive the benefit of a support group requires taking the first move. Why not get one started now? You could contact persons with similar situations in your denomination. Or you might test interest across denominational lines. The main issue is to recognize that someone like you is already coping, and they can help you understand how God intends for you to move beyond family endurance to enjoyment.

● *Keep Yourself in Parental Training for Life*
An effective parent never stops learning, regardless of years in ministry or the age of children. When church or society presents a new problem, the person in training begins to seek ways to master it with God's enablement. Like an athlete in training, this effort keeps one alert, energetic, and in top mental condition—ready to win.

No need to feel locked in to what has happened in your family, but dare to believe what can be. Accept and use the fact that new problems lurking around critical issues often lead to deeper understandings and renewed relationships. In the process, you can discover the answers you do not now have and enrich your family relationships.

### THE CONTEMPORARY CHALLENGE
### ALLOW YOUR FAMILY TO NOURISH YOUR MINISTRY

Let's change the mood in clergy families from worry to support, from surviving to thriving, and from self-pity to winsome satisfaction. Such an overcoming strategy calls you to love and be loved by family, so the most significant people in your life nourish your inner spring.

Allow the quality of your family relationships to transform your home into a sanctuary where love, acceptance, affirmation, and accountability recharge your spiritual and emotional batteries. Use family togetherness to renew your whole being and to enrich each other.

Resist competition between family and ministry. Make them complementary and mutually beneficial. God intended them to supplement, enrich, and nourish each other.

Then during compelling demands of ministry, turn your heart toward home where love, support, intimacy, and friendship await you. Make your family the most significant people in your life. Most churches want you to give your family a high place in your affections, priorities, and values.

Every pastor needs his family's love fully as much as he needs a strong church to strengthen his ministry.

The miracle of family religion enriches your life and empowers your service for Christ.

**RENEWAL STRATEGIES**
**HELPING PKS STAY WELL-ADJUSTED**

✔ *Please the People Who Matter Most*
✔ *Get Your Family in Tune with God*
✔ *Feed Faith to Children*
✔ *Refuse to Blame Problems on the Ministry*
✔ *View Family As a Gift from God*
✔ *Focus on the Present*
✔ *Start a Family Support Group*
✔ *Keep Yourself in Parental Training for Life*

SIX

# We Suffer Alone
# with Money Problems

"Our family is the only one in the congregation that lives below the poverty line." — a pastor's daughter from Arkansas

We pastors have no way to dicker about money and few ways to earn extra bucks. Our financial decisions are made by governing groups who have no firsthand knowledge of our money pressures. We suffer alone; there is no acceptable way to tell anyone." That is how Pastor Barth Mills describes his economic woes.

He is right. A pastor may be considered greedy if he discusses family financial problems with church members. If he shares his financial woes with a denominational supervisor or bishop, leaders may question his ability to manage money, his own or the church's. And no one wants a preacher to trumpet his bills from the pulpit. No acceptable way exists to communicate these problems to anyone who could change them.

## Pastors' Income and Expense Are Unique
Earning and spending issues are much different for pastors than other professionals, business owners, tradespeople, factory workers, or employees at McDonalds™.

Doctors and lawyers raise fees when inflation accelerates or insurance premiums go up. Teachers can move up the pay scale by taking classes, coaching, or teaching summer school. Business owners elevate earnings by increasing markups, selling more units, or working longer hours. Tradespeople can increase their hourly rates by developing new skills, increasing bids, or negotiating union contracts. Even McDonalds'™ workers receive increases when minimum wage laws are changed or when they work extra hours.

**RISK FACTORS**

70% of pastors in a 1992 survey indicated that their compensation contributed to conflict in their marriage.

*Leadership,* Fall 1992

None of these possibilities exist for pastors. They have no fees to boost, no financial incentives for completing college courses, no raises for tenure, no extra pay for overtime, no goods to mark up, no new units to sell, and no hourly rates to increase by skills, contract, or union negotiations.

Instead, clergy compensation is usually determined by church budgets, by lay leaders' vision, or by tradition/custom. Inflation rates and merit raises are frequently ignored or debated negatively in the church. Decisions about ministers' salaries are oftentimes interfaced with housing arrangements, utilities costs, and automobile expenses.

Today, pastors encounter more financial jeopardy than ever before. Symptoms include working wives and bi-vocational jobs, plus the skyrocketing costs of medical insurance, college tuition, and car expenses.

**Money Problems As Pastors View Them**
Many urgent letters from pastors reveal near desperate financial pressures. Many clergy families live with a constant financial panic.

• A pastor from Alaska: "I am being pressured out of the ministry by a constant financial juggling act."

• A pastoral staff member from St. Louis: "We feel pressure to live a lifestyle that is commonly accepted in an affluent society. Long-term, this strain affects my whole view of ministry."

• A senior pastor from Seattle: "Our situation requires a working wife for us to keep our heads above the water. Some in the church feel we could be better money managers, but they earn almost twice as much as our combined family income."

• A youth pastor from Georgia: "Our challenge is to live within our income and still not embarrass the church with the kind of clothes we wear and the car we drive. I am not talking extravagant, just respectable."

• A veteran pastor from Cleveland: "Many younger pastors have school and seminary expenses which hover over their heads, so one income will not possibly see them through. Their financial pressure is so great many leave the ministry because they are not able to make ends meet."

• A pastor from the Midwest: "My wife is bitter toward the church because she feels they have stolen a reasonable standard of living from us."

• A pastor from Rhode Island: "I am forty-nine years old, have three children that I cannot afford to send to any college, drive a used car, and hope to save enough for retirement."

• A minister's wife from Indiana: "Because of a huge split in the church, our bishop suggested that Bob take an outside job. He did, and in three short years he is now manager of his department plus pastoring. The

> **RISK FACTORS**
>
> 22% of pastors in one survey feel forced to supplement their church income.
>
> *Leadership*, Fall 1992

church still cannot afford hospital insurance or a full salary, so Bob feels he has to keep this job for the benefits. His work schedule puts unbelievable pressure on our family, marriage, and church."

## How One Pastor Dealt with Personal Financial Debt: Interview with Gary Allen

Pastor Gary Allen, age forty-five, father of four children, grew up in Texas and graduated with an engineering degree from

Texas A & M University. After ten years with General Electric, he was called into ministry as a second career and went to Dallas Seminary. He has served in his first pastorate at the First Evangelical Free Church in Cedar Falls, Iowa, for the past nine years.

Allen preached a sermon series on the Christian's use of money in which he openly shared his own struggles and victories. A member of his church sent a cassette of the sermon to Focus on the Family. This following interview came as a result of that contact.

**London/Wiseman:** Pastor Allen, thanks for sharing your story. How did you get into financial difficulty, and how is your situation different from other pastors who live on modest incomes?

**Allen:** It was the result of several factors. We charged things we were not willing to wait for, like a computer, and we had monthly charge accounts like Sears, plus our credit cards.

**London/Wiseman:** Lots of people who are not in ministry have similar problems.

**Allen:** Two additional factors compounded our predicament. The first was medical bills from my oldest son's moped accident. A car hit him and he was in the hospital for six weeks. After the insurance paid, we still owed $3,000. And we had other medical expenses that piled up on top of the hospital bill.

The other problem started with a stupid decision. In order to catch up on our income taxes, I charged over $3,000 on Visa and Mastercard, maxing them to the limit. Of course, that postponed my problem for a short while, but it eventually made things much worse because of the interest charges.

**London/Wiseman:** This problem ticking like a time bomb, then, was an accumulation of debt, charge accounts, income taxes, medical bills, and credit cards charged to the limit?

**Allen:** Yes, and I learned the hard way that there is no pressure like financial pressures for a pastor. We suffered for several months with the tremendous burden of facing these bills without enough money to pay even the minimum payments.

Then we started shuffling the bills to pay one and let the other one go. Then we got calls from creditors. It just went from bad to worse.

What turned the corner for us was when I was preaching from Proverbs last year and came across two passages that really stuck out to me. The passages are Proverbs 3:5-6 and 6:1-5. The first asks us to trust the Lord with all our heart. And three chapters later, the second passage instructs us what to do when we get in debt and how to get out.

**London/Wiseman:** So you were helped by your own preaching? That might be a useful resource for all of us who preach.

**Allen:** As I studied and preached, the Lord seemed to say, "Are you going to trust Me? Are you going to solve this problem My way or yours?"

## Steps out of Debt
**London/Wiseman:** What specific steps did you take?

**Allen:** I started with Proverbs 6:1-5. The steps are spelled out: go, humble yourself, and importune your neighbor. I understood this meant I was to go to the people to whom we were indebted, to humble myself, and to lay out our situation as succinctly as possible. It is embarrassing to admit you have made a financial mess of your life and to admit you do not know any way out unless the creditors help you. The word "importune" means begging or pleading for mercy. So I did those very things.

First, I made a list of all my creditors, how much I owed them, and how far behind I was. In every case, it was two or three months. I had a total of thirteen creditors, and my total debt was $9,244. I was over $1,500 behind in my payments.

So I made that list and wrote to each creditor. I said to them, "You can see the size of my problem from the enclosed sheet."

Before writing them, I determined that I could pay $20 per month on each bill. That was all. That amount sounded ridiculous to me because my minimum payments on Visa and Mastercard were $60 to $75 per month.

In the letter to each creditor, I laid out the situation and gave them a listing of my debts. I told them it was my desire to pay them off and to get out of debt. My plan was to start at the $20 level to each creditor. And then, as the lowest debt was paid off, I would roll that $20 over into the next higher debt.

**London/Wiseman:** What response did you get?

**Allen:** I asked in my letter if I could have some relief from the interest because if I paid $20 per month on Visa and Mastercard, my interest charges were almost that much. I did not know what to expect since compassion and caring are not the first things that come into my mind when I think about credit card companies — they are in business to make money.

But they called and said they were willing to go with the plan, allowing me to pay $20 a month. And they were willing not to charge more interest during this period when I was trying to pay everything off.

**London/Wiseman:** How did the hospital answer?

**Allen:** At the time I wrote, we owed $2,264. They accepted my repayment plan and wrote off $1,795 as an act of goodwill to help with our financial burdens. So instead of $2,264, I only owed $448, which I paid off at $20 per month.

**London/Wiseman:** How much time have you been involved in reducing your debt?

**Allen:** It has been almost one year to this date. When I wrote those letters, I owed $9,244. Today I owe $4,593. I figured when I wrote those letters that it would take me about 36 months to get everything paid off.

## Family Agreement

**London/Wiseman:** What is the most difficult aspect of this whole process? Does your family understand the dilemma that they might not be able to have every new tennis shoe that comes out, a new car, or the latest computer?

**Allen:** My wife and I worked together on this; she was in full agreement. And the children have been willing to go along and make adjustments.

**London/Wiseman:** If you could be a pastor to pastors, what would you say to fellow ministers who find themselves overspending and living beyond their means?

**Allen:** Three things really matter about this new life of financial responsibility and freedom. The first is to trust in the Lord in all financial aspects of life. I had to get to the point where I was convicted that I was in a mess that was displeasing to God.

**London/Wiseman:** So there is the foundational spiritual dimension.

**Allen:** The second issue comes from Proverbs 3:9 where we are instructed to give the Lord the first of our produce. I remember Howard Hendricks saying that it is not what you do with a million if a million is not your lot, but what you do with the buck and a quarter you have in your pocket now.

And then third, the word of encouragement is clear in Proverbs 6 about the process of getting out of debt.

**London/Wiseman:** Thanks for sharing your financial journey. We are grateful for your advice. Your story will help other pastors see how they can get better control of their limited funds.

## How a Minister Masters Money Management

Hundreds of pastors like Gary Allen struggle every month to keep from drowning in a sea of money problems. They feel imprisoned by low salaries, high expenses, limited financial know-how and heavy debt. Real help is needed. Following is an interview with financial adviser and author Ron Blue who offers solid strategies pastors can use to untangle confusing money matters.

### Interview with Ron Blue
**London/Wiseman:** We've heard you know a pastor who retired with a million dollars. Did you really mean a million? Your story has us stunned. Did it actually happen?

**Blue:** The story is true. I know a pastor who retired with 1 million dollars, and others could also do remarkably well.

**London/Wiseman:** Think how that figure boggles the mind of a pastor who earns $15,000 a year or less. Do you know their typical situation? They have a couple of teenagers at home and a son in college. Their car is six years old, so they have all kinds of maintenance in front of them. They want to go away to celebrate their twenty-fifth anniversary, but they do not have enough money. Now how do they identify with a million dollars?

**Blue:** After I wrote that illustration, I met with that pastor again to ask him how he did it. He gave me the basic financial principles he practiced.

He always tithed first.

I asked if he ever borrowed money, and he replied, "No, I never could afford to borrow any money." I followed up with my question, "Well, what do you mean you could not afford to borrow money?" Listen to his answer: "I always felt if I borrowed money, I would have to pay it back, and I could not afford to pay it back."

So the second idea after his tithe, he never borrowed money.

The third thing, he always lived with a budget and within his income. Although he never made a lot of money, by the time he retired he had accumulated a nest egg that had really grown to be a large sum of money.

## What about Nest Eggs?

London/Wiseman: Let us consider money conditions for most ministers for a minute. If they have one, their nest eggs are never very large. Pastors simply do not have much firsthand experience with a nest egg.

Blue: A nest egg is nothing more than a little bit of savings or a little bit of a retirement account. This pastor with the million dollars started by doing all that he could do with what he had. But he kept doing what he could. He did not try to strike it rich in investments, oil, or anything else. He did what he could to add to the nest egg, and it multiplied over time.

The starting point is to do what you can with what you have. I believe that if you set aside $5 a week, $20 a month, or whatever it may be, then you are doing what you can in order to provide for an uncertain economic future.

London/Wiseman: A key thing you said earlier about this particular pastor was that he tithed faithfully.

Blue: Absolutely. Many people miss the important issue that the tithe is pivotal because it tends to put the right priority on a person's use of money. Typically, the American family looks at the tithe as something that they will do if they have a surplus, and nobody ever has a surplus.

London/Wiseman: That's a riveting issue dealing with personal finance, but it also impacts a pastor's preaching about stewardship. Like you said, tithing puts the right priority on our use of money.

There is another concern for pastors that nobody talks about much. Pastors give lots of money; sometimes they give when they cannot afford it.

Blue: What do you mean?

London/Wiseman: Some give 20 or 25 percent of their income to the church. Though they do not begrudge that in any way, over the years it amounts to a lot of money.

How about the minister's wife who sees at the end of the

month how much her husband has given to the church? Neither of them can believe how much money it is. Then she reminds him, "You know the kids need shoes. The car needs tires. You haven't had a new suit for two years. And I've been wearing the same old dresses to church every Sunday for the last six months."

What do we say to those situations? Often she is a sacrificial financial partner in the family who works outside her home to help meet the family budget.

**Blue:** I think there is something bigger than finance here. The bigger issue is communication about money. I believe that a husband and wife, be they pastors, physicians, or businesspeople, need to have monetary communication so they make joint decisions on tithing, borrowing, budgeting, vacations, and other expenditures. Neither one should dictate to the other.

So I think what you have said is a problem of the pastor not getting good agreement with his spouse in making those decisions.

**London/Wiseman:** But these difficulties usually do not show up until after the money is given.

**Blue:** That's an important point. The conversation should take place at the beginning of the month before the decision is made.

## The Meaning of Money
**London/Wiseman:** Do you have definite suggestions?

**Blue:** Let me try. There are only five things you can do with money: (1) you can give it—which is the tithe; (2) you can spend it; (3) you can save it for future needs; (4) you can pay off your debts; and (5) you can pay your taxes.

Only two things in that list are mandatory—taxes and debt repayment. The first three are discretionary, and how you allocate them is a result of your priorities.

We Suffer Alone with Money Problems

**London/Wiseman:** What are the appropriate priorities for pastors?

**Blue:** The same as everyone else. When it comes to making money priority decisions, you tithe first, save second, pay your taxes, pay off your debt, and live off the rest. I think that puts the right priority into money management.

**London/Wiseman:** As a financial adviser and counselor, what do you say to pastors about taxes? How can their advantages be used wisely?

**Blue:** When it comes to pastors, there is a tax advantage on the housing allowance which is a nontaxable receipt of income that is probably the best there can be.

Other than that, a pastor has the same opportunities relative to tax advantages that anybody else would have, such as an IRA or retirement account and tax-sheltered annuities. A pastor can take up to 16 percent of his income and put it into a tax-sheltered annuity whether or not the church participates in it—that is a tremendous tax advantage. There is no other retirement program like that one, and it is exceedingly advantageous for a pastor.

**London/Wiseman:** Many pastors do not get involved in a tax-sheltered program because they say to themselves, "With our bills and with our financial commitments, we just cannot afford to do that kind of thing."

**Blue:** I think you are right. They feel overwhelmed by money worries. But I would challenge the assumption that they cannot afford to be involved in some level of tax-sheltered annuities. I question their conclusion until the pastor and his spouse have done some serious financial planning. Like the millionaire minister-retiree, a little amount saved often is the way to care for the future.

**London/Wiseman:** But ministers do not believe they can afford to save, and their bills prove their point.

**Blue**: They need a plan for the money they have rather than having no plan for what they do not have. The question is how are they going to allocate their dollars among the alternatives. Remember, there are only five choices: (1) give, (2) spend, (3) save, (4) pay off debt, or (5) pay taxes. If they wait for extra money to come out of what is left at the end of the month, that almost never happens. You have to preplan savings or it never takes place. I think you have to preplan your giving or it won't happen.

**London/Wiseman**: Illustrate that idea so we can see it plainly.

**Blue**: Let me try. If you could save $83 a month, that is $1,000 a year on a $20,000 income, or 5 percent. If you save $1,000 a year over a working life of forty years, from age twenty-five to sixty-five, you would have saved $40,000. You could put that $40,000 away, $1,000 a year, in a tax-sheltered annuity. Then if you were able to grow that $40,000 at the rate of 12 1/2 percent per year, $1,000 saved per year, or $83 a month, would grow to 1 million dollars over a forty-year time period. So you would save $40,000 and end up with a million, and there would have been no taxes paid on that.

You say I cannot get 12 1/2 percent, but if you can get half of that interest rate, you can end up with $500,000. At 6 1/4 percent, you have half a million dollars saved over a forty-year time period.

**London/Wiseman**: But what about money management mistakes. Pastors make mistakes partially because they have so little experience with personal finance. You may have made a few errors yourself—maybe that is why you wrote the book.

**Blue**: Absolutely!

## Dealing with Debt
**London/Wiseman**: Pastors do not have the luxury of making too many mistakes because their income is so low.

Let us give you a scenario. A pastor goes to college and gets married, so when husband and wife graduate there are usually two college debts. Then they go to seminary. Seminary is very expensive now. So they come out of seminary owing college bills plus seminary debt. That is a huge investment that pastors did not have to deal with twenty-five years ago. Some couples owe as much as $30,000 and then take a small church that pays a minimum beginning salary.

**Blue:** When you start out with that college debt, it is going to take a long time to repay it. That may be a reality, however, to many pastors now. Let me give you three points in dealing with debt.

*First,* they must define reality. Don't kid yourself; most people who are in debt do not want to deal with it. By defining reality, I mean listing everything you owe and what the payments are. Do not kid yourself. Total it up. Talk about it. Admit it to each other.

The *second* step is to begin a repayment plan. Even if it is a minimal repayment plan, get yourself under some disciplined plan — $100 a month, $200 a month, or whatever it may be. But start repaying.

A *third* point is that you stop going into debt. Quit borrowing money. Stop using credit cards.

Then let's add a *fourth* point of making yourself accountable to someone. That is going to be difficult for a pastor because it is tough for anybody, but it will be especially hard for a highly visible spiritual leader.

That is the process for dealing with debt — you define reality, set up a repayment plan, stop going into debt, and hold yourself accountable to somebody to get out of that debt. Those four points is the way to settle the problem.

**London/Wiseman:** That is great advice. Undoubtedly, pastors experience subtle anger about money because their incomes are low, and they feel they have no alternative but to go into debt.

**Blue:** Let's talk about that. We have a fellow who works for me who has been paid a nice income in his present job. Recently, he decided that God has called him to do mission work in Moscow. In this move, his income is going to be a third of what it is now. Yet when we talk about it, I've said, "Look, if God called you to that particular assignment in that particular location, then He is the one who is also providing the income for you. Then it is not an issue of having more income, but of living within the income that God has provided for you."

**London/Wiseman:** But that is not always easy. Pretend for a moment that you are reading this letter from a pastor's wife who is discouraged because of her financial situation: "Pastors' families need all the help, encouragement, and hope they can lay their hands on. So often we are asked to give all our finances, our time, our energies, our homes, our families, to sacrifice, if need be, because we are called of God. We are asked to live on little. And people say to us, 'Oh, God will provide; you are the pastor.' We've heard this time and time again."

That pastor's wife probably has the responsibility of balancing the family budget at the end of the month. She has lots of reasons for feeling the way she does. And she certainly does not need to be judged as not being spiritual because she is weary of carrying this heavy load so long.

**Blue:** I really empathize with her because I think she expresses the feeling of thousands of pastors' wives.

I do not have a financial solution to that one because there isn't any. Without question, the lay leaders of that church are going to be held accountable for how they treated the Lord's servants. I would hate to stand before our Lord as a deacon or an elder in that particular church.

But since the pastor does not have control of what the lay leaders decide, I believe this minister's family has to do everything they can to live within the income they have. Doing that takes more than anger and pain.

**London/Wiseman:** One final thing—it is often said that if everybody would just tithe, we would not have any financial problems in the church. We wouldn't even have to have debt reduction programs and that kind of thing. How do you see it?

**Blue**: I'm convinced, however much or little one has, that giving is a spiritual decision and not an economic decision. So we are really talking about the spiritual heartbeat of people as opposed to the economic heartbeat. And what you said is exactly right. I am becoming more persuaded every day that there is more than enough money right now to fulfill the Great Commission if people knew that they could, should, and would give it. It is not a lack of money, but a lack of obedience.

## A Low-Risk Guide to Coping with Financial Doldrums

Though money problems worry ministers perpetually, Ron Blue and Gary Allen have suggested several useful ways of viewing pastors' money difficulties. The majority of these difficulties are a result of existing church budgeting structures. Even though tradition says it is the church's responsibility to care for the pastor, few do it adequately. And there are many inaccurate myths among lay leaders about ministers and money.

In defense of thousands of conscientious lay leaders, they think they adequately compensate their pastor without ever factually considering his housing and education needs or the relationship of money to his feelings of self-worth. Too many salary decisions are based on traditions and emotions rather than on fact and need.

> ### RISK FACTORS
>
> In the last 3 years the typical pastor's salary has increased less than half the inflation rate, according to a recent survey by Christianity Today, Inc. The average increase for 1988–1991 was only 7.4%. Over 40% of the single-staff pastors and 33% of senior ministers said they felt they were underpaid.
>
> *Current Thoughts & Trends,*
> May 1992

Some emotional relief comes from a change in the clergy couple's perspective and resulting actions. However, such a change in viewpoint is not easily achieved because clergy tend to blame salary difficulties on stingy gremlins beyond their control.

Admittedly, salaries in most churches are too low, but in a few situations the couple's viewpoint is the problem. They need to know if their money plight is a reality or the result of mismanagement. To sort through these issues, questions might be asked about average family income in the community; salary paid by the same size church in the next town, county, and state; or the church's financial capability to increase the salary. They must also take a hard look at the financial implications of benefits, such as housing, utilities, and insurance premiums, which often make the church's financial provisions significantly larger than the stated cash salary.

Mickey and Ashmore spark another surprising issue in their book *Clergy Families — Is Normal Life Possible?* Their research supports an inverse correlation between calling and salary: "The clearer the call, the fewer the complaints; and income is less frequently the measure of ministry. For those pastors whose sense of vocation is not so sharp, finances become a measure of personal worth and affect self-esteem."[1] Most pastors have never thought about such a relationship.

At least three money issues recur in pastors' letters. *Income size* is the first — salaries are grossly inadequate when compared with other professionals. Is that comparison useful?

The second issue is *lifestyle* — simply being involved in ministry seems to dictate a middle-class living standard which includes dressing well, giving children as many opportunities as possible, eating out, entertaining, plus owning late-model automobiles.

*Debt costs* is the third factor impacting ministers' family budgets — money spent to service loans robs dollars from other needs and family wants. These concerns are underscored in a pastor's wife's comment: "We are accustomed to nice things and fine furniture. It is hard for us to live on a salary that is commensurate with the size and financial strength of our church because we both came from middle-income business families."

128

## New Ways of Looking at Money

Two questions trouble pastors: Will I ever have enough money? and Does my congregation know that our family's financial well-being is in their hands?

These are tricky issues between church and pastor. Think of the possible pitfalls. Many churches have restricted incomes. Pastors, because of taste and education, tend to prefer a middle-class lifestyle. The people whom the pastor serves are often the ones who make official decisions about his income and benefits. And a pastor has almost no way to negotiate improvements.

Everyone in the pastor's wide sphere of influence is harmed if unrealistic financial expectations from any source become wet wood on the fire of the minister's devotion. Therefore, a pastor might want to use one or more of the following new ways of looking at money to keep financial matters in perspective. At any cost, he must keep economic worries from locking him into bad feelings toward systems and decision-makers.

● *Earn a Raise through the Father's Praise*

"Money makes folks funny," observed a wise old pastor we know. He is so right. Sooner or later, blaming and complaining about money disgusts everyone in a congregation or community. Unfortunately, some pastors, without intending to do so, allow themselves to become experts at badgering or insinuating about money. Even subtle manipulations are resented by some.

However, our personal attitude toward a modest salary always improves when we remember for whom we ultimately work. God's praise is a mighty high payoff, much more desirable than money.

Why not do ministry so well that you know God is pleased? Meanwhile, one of His servants in a decision group might remind the others, "We need to increase our pastor's salary because he is serving people so well."

Seeking the Father's praise is likely to keep a pastor's vision clear and permeate his ministry with meaning even when raises seem slow in coming. Judge your ministry by the effect it has on those God has called you to serve.

● *Come to Terms with a Two-Income Society*
The traditional model of the pastor's wife not working outside her home is falling by the wayside fast. Like it or not, contemporary society is built on two-family incomes. And even though pastors may resist this reality or even preach against it, it is here to stay.

This means that when the pastor's wife chooses not to work outside the home, the family will have a lower standard of living than many parishioners. The resulting nitty-gritty frustrations should not be blamed on the church or on women in the congregation who choose another route. Such a choice by the pastor's wife has a price tag, as well as many possible nonfinancial benefits.

A reversed kind of realism should also be applied to the extra income earned by bi-vocational pastors. Is such work outside the church to be a continuing source of financial support or is it a temporary supplement? What pressures does such an arrangement place on the family and ministry? And what happens if the job is lost?

● *Check Wants against Goals*
Do we really need or even want what we buy? Ron Blue makes a powerful observation: "When we choose to believe that something or someone will meet our needs, we make foolish financial decisions leading to debt. . . . When we believe we are secure and significant, nothing needs to be added to our lives to increase our contentment. Yet most of our activities, financial and nonfinancial, revolve around trying to satisfy those needs."[2]

Most purchases are rooted more in emotional and social issues than in actual needs. This fact makes it important that we keep trying to understand the real reasons behind our purchasing patterns.

Though it is easy to forget in this culture, our significance and security are built on our relationship with God and not on the size of our paycheck, the price of our car, or the number of credit cards we have.

● *Keep God First*
It sounds so simple, but keeping God in top priority is not easy in our kind of world. So much of what we hear and see encourages us to forget that believers march to a different drummer.

Though we fear financial downtimes, much of the faith formation literature teaches it may be spiritually invigorating to be stretched by pressing money woes so we remember that we live by a different value system than the world. Absolute dependence on God is one of the most satisfying characteristics of a Christian.

Ron Blue's advice in the interview must be heard above all our modern clamor about money, "Many people miss the important issue that the tithe is pivotal because it tends to put the right priority on a person's use of money."

Let's remember the Bible clearly teaches that greed tempts every individual regardless of their income, and generosity toward God and human needs is its remedy.

● *Preach on Money*
Wrestling with money concepts from Scripture and sharing those discoveries with a congregation helps everyone. Such an encounter furnishes a pastor with a healthy self-test for his own stewardship and beliefs about ownership; preaching to oneself often challenges us to improvement and wholeness.

Never before in Christian history have so many print and audiovisual materials been available to help believers maximize their use of financial resources. These books and tapes, often built on biblical principles, can be used to inform the preacher's preaching on the subject and later shared with members of the congregation. Two recent books on the Christian's use of money topped the Christian bestseller list for months—a fact that demonstrates an increased interest among believers in this subject.

● *Get Control of Debt*

The money you save and the peace of mind you experience from getting free of debt are enormous benefits for ministers. Freedom from debt provides a higher standard of living in your future and frees you from continuous financial strains. The interviews with Gary Allen and Ron Blue offer specific strategies for beating the debt squeeze so many pastors feel.

Let the strongest possible warning be sounded to pastors everywhere—misused debt destroys ministry. The demolition comes either from the pastors' inner world of worry and frustration or from without in the congregation or community. Then too excessive debt can also shut down the pastor's creative forces.

● *Resist Comparisons*

Coveting, comparisons, and competition sabotage ministry. Envy is a cancer of the spirit that slowly ravages spiritual health—even envy of the pastor's salary in the next town. The Apostle Paul offered magnificent modeling when he testified of being content with what he had.

But it is the American way to keep track of the cost of the neighbor's house, car, and clothes. It is a stupid sacrilege and a waste of time. No one has ever gotten one more penny by begrudging another's possessions, but lots of people have lost their souls or developed a selfish spirit over the issue.

Everyone is rich in some way, including you. No one else has your unique relationship with God, your happy marriage, your smart kids, your faith, or the love of the people in your church.

Pastors should avoid comparing compensations because it leads down an emotional and spiritual dead-end street. No one has all the facts. No one has all the costs. No one knows why one pastor gets better pay than another. Thus, even when there is gross inequity, spending energy on these issues seldom solves anything. And it usually makes the person doing the comparing more perplexed or more dissatisfied about his own situation.

132

We Suffer Alone with Money Problems

● *Keep Free from Possession Fixations*
Society says to moderns, "Do be possessed by your possessions." The advice is excellent because many buy bigger houses to hold stuff they never use. Still others are so afraid someone will steal what they have accumulated that they guard their possessions with big guns, vicious dogs, or sophisticated alarm systems.

Though most pastors never feel those problems, many experience the exact opposite. They are enslaved by possessions they do not have. This kind of invisible slavery steals their happiness and puts deep tired lines in their faces.

Listen closely to what Jesus says: "Watch out! Be on your guard against all kinds of greed; a man's life does not consist in the abundance of his possessions" (Luke 12:15).

## THE CONTEMPORARY CHALLENGE
### REST IN GOD'S FAITHFULNESS

God's sufficiency is the foundation for faithful ministry today and for the future. On page after page, the Bible teaches the absolute faithfulness of God—He is the dependable one. Though wholehearted dependence on the most reliable human being can be risky business, God never lets us down. And He is responsible for supplying our needs wherever He places us. That includes your present assignment.

Pastorates seldom pay as much as a pastor would like to receive. But polls taken in other occupations show that few people in any line of work believe they are paid enough, and even fewer consider the possibility that they might be overpaid. Ministers are like that too. One pastor's joking line is true: "I have been overpaid in every church, but it has never been more than I needed to live on."

God's faithfulness, as dependable as the rising of tomorrow's sun, is the beyond-sufficiency component that must be factored into our concerns about security and money. John Wesley gave good advice: earn all you can, give all you can, and save all you can.

133

**RENEWAL STRATEGIES**
## DEALING WITH THE MONEY STRUGGLE

- *Earn a Raise through the Father's Praise*
- *Come to Terms with a Two-Income Society*
- *Check Wants against Goals*
- *Keep God First*
- *Preach on Money*
- *Get Control of Debt*
- *Resist Comparisons*
- *Keep Free from Possession Fixations*

# SEVEN

# Who Is This Superwoman by the Pastor's Side?

"Parsonage women, let nothing come between you and that man of yours. No busyness of yours or his, no project, no building, no committee, no assignment—nothing!"—from a minister's wife in Colorado

T he work of the church is much too complicated for a pastor alone. Now, as much as ever, the church depends on the minister's wife for energy and imagination. And increasingly, in many churches, pastors' wives work outside the home as well, bearing financial burdens in addition to all they carry in their hearts.

The whirlwind of women's issues that appear so often in print and on TV has pastors' wives reeling as they strain to cope with marriage, children, career, and church. The highly visible issues of the women's movement prompt them to examine old questions about ministry in new and different ways: What about work outside my home? What about those frustrating expectations—others and mine? What about my husband's long work hours? What about money for pressing needs? Will my children survive the stress?

Though no pat answers are available, pastors' wives need to face these issues and answer these questions to their own satisfaction.

## The Contemporary Scene

Dr. James C. Dobson recently noted that about 5 percent of the letters received at Focus on the Family come from pastors' wives. In H.B.'s office, the figure increases to 20 percent because he especially serves pastors and their families. In their letters, pastors' wives share frustrations that run the gamut from loneliness to anger. These concerns are rooted in the changing nature of ministry and the risks that pastors and their families face.

**RISK FACTORS**

60% of clergy wives hold full-time jobs or are involved in careers.
Malony and Hunt, *The Psychology of Clergy*

We invited Linda Riley, an active pastor's wife, to share ways pastors' wives can survive joyfully in partnership with their husbands. Riley established and continues to lead a support service for pastors' wives, Called Together Ministries, located in Torrance, California, which publishes a referral directory, *Guide to Support Resources for Clergy*.

## Interview with Linda Riley

**London/Wiseman**: Thanks for allowing us to walk into your important ministry to pastors' wives. First, tell us about your family.

**Riley**: Jay, my wonderful husband, and I have been together in ministry for nineteen years. We have four children: the youngest is a boy and three older girls. We serve a small independent suburban church in Torrance, California. Our church has about 140 adults and lots of children.

**London/Wiseman**: Share some details about your ministry for women who are married to pastors.

**Riley**: Called Together Ministries is a service to pastors' wives. I understand them because I am one. Notice I say pastors' wives rather than spouses because more than 90 percent of pastors in the United States are male. Concerns of men who are married to clergywomen are so different from pastors' wives that I could not possibly address both groups.

**London/Wiseman:** That's a good point. Could you describe your own faith journey? When you think of your life in ministry, is it much different than you expected when you and your husband started?

**Riley:** I was young when we started—twenty-one—and I remember having a prideful feeling of self-importance. I recall thinking it was a privilege and a challenge to be married to a pastor. But I was so alarmingly naive. Though for my age I knew much about God, I knew very little about people. I needed better understanding of people's emotional makeup; they can be so strange and unpredictable. In ministry, it is important to understand them.

**London/Wiseman:** There is no school for pastors' wives, is there?

**Riley:** No, but there are a lot of books out there—some helpful and some not. And many Bible schools and seminaries are now developing courses for ministers' wives.

## Mentors for Pastors' Wives
**London/Wiseman:** In the early years did you have a mentor or model? Was there a pastor's wife from whom you could draw encouragement or guidance?

**Riley:** Yes, the pastor's wife in the church where I first became a Christian. I was saved during the Jesus Movement in 1970, in a congregation led by a pastor who used to be a Kansas farmer. He was as different as night and day from the hippies who came to get saved in his church. And his wife was caring and sweet. Though the situation of dealing with people so unlike them must have been confusing, they just stood back and let God do wonderful things in that little church.

**London/Wiseman:** What was helpful about that pastor's wife?

**Riley:** Let me explain a little more fully. Those were fruitful days of harvest; young people would fall on their knees when the name "Jesus" was mentioned. In that setting, the pastor's wife was sort of an old-fashioned type—always lovable and interested. She was very noncontroversial and supportive of everyone, especially her husband. For me, she was a wonderful example of a strong Christian woman. We still maintain a friendship with her.

I'd like to add that I am impressed by almost every pastor's wife I know. They all have commendable strengths, chiefly, perseverance, dedication, commitment, and a desire to please the Lord and to serve their families and churches. For the most part, they have risen to meet the challenges of ministry life and are a great asset to their churches and communities.

### Is Help Available?

**London/Wiseman:** Where do pastors' wives go for help if they do not have such a model? Is that the reason you started Called Together Ministries?

**Riley:** Called Together Ministries started out of my own sense of futility. As I mentioned, our little church came up in the Jesus Movement with many young people. With our tremendous numerical growth, many crisis situations arose where we had to help people, like getting kids off drugs. But the work was rewarding, and it is easy to endure trials when you see spiritual fruit. Our problems were mostly with new converts and had little to do with church difficulties. So, due to our unique situation, my life was sheltered during that first decade from problems in ministry.

But then things drastically changed about eight years ago. Our senior pastor had a nervous breakdown. It might be called burnout now. He suddenly became totally unable to function and had to be hospitalized. He later committed suicide, and that was tough for our church to absorb. Consequently, some people lost out, and we had a church split. About the same time, we also had an unrelated lawsuit with accompanying unfavorable publicity.

**London/Wiseman:** What happened then?

**Riley:** That was a devastating time for us. My husband and I felt so alone. Since we ministered in an independent church, we had not taken the time to build relationships with pastors in the area. Mistakenly, we did not go to ministerial fellowships nor attend weekly prayer meetings for pastors.

That changed immediately. As soon as our problems hit, our tentacles went out fast, searching for friendship and help. We started building up a support network immediately. We also received some counseling from a local church that helped us, even though we were not part of their denomination. Then we finally sought professional counseling to get us through the emotional hurts of the church split.

**London/Wiseman:** So Called Together Ministries grew out of your own struggles?

**Riley:** The main motivation for starting Called Together Ministries was an unproductive search for help for myself. I went to seminary libraries and Christian bookstores to find print resources to get me through this ordeal. And when I found material, I often wasted time reading books that skirted the issue or did not address the leader's point of view. I realized from painful experience that it is difficult to find what you need when you need it most.

We had a similar experience when we tried to locate resources to assist our senior pastor when he had his breakdown. I had heard of ministries to ministers but had a tough time finding them.

That is when Called Together Ministries started in my mind. I thought there should be some resource organization so when a pastor and/or his wife are in trouble, they can call to find exactly what they need. So we started with a book and tape catalog and then developed a referral network. Later I added a listening line to offer reassurance and prayer. But all we do is just a Band-Aid™ compared to what many people need. So we see our ministry as being able to introduce them to resources where they can go to receive more intensive help.

**London/Wiseman:** Are you saying, don't be a lone ranger? Don't try to fight the battles alone, but go for help where somebody understands what you are feeling.

**Riley:** Yes. The need for this type of help is especially important now because of the increasing number of broken families, single-parent homes, and escalating use of drugs and alcohol. Think of the effect those conditions will have on future ministries. It will also be more pressing in ministers' families because many more people now going into ministry are from troubled families, and they have unresolved personal issues from their own backgrounds. And more dysfunctional people will be coming into churches.

**London/Wiseman:** Family crises in the minister's personal life and the church are increasing rapidly, and somebody has to do something about it.

**Riley:** The problems are coming faster than we can imagine. We will have more issues, more turmoil, and more broken people who want to work out their personal problems in church settings. Pastors will need more support. I know from putting a guide together that we need many more support services.

## Loneliness Is an Overwhelming Problem

**London/Wiseman:** Can we move now to more detailed concerns and possible solutions. What are the main problems you hear from pastors' wives?

**Riley:** Loneliness is the number one problem. Many pastors' wives have been taught they cannot make friends within their own church. Others decide, after being disappointed by gossip, that they have been a little too open and draw back at a time when they are hungry for friendships. As you know, women need close friendships, and they need a confidant.

Especially in rural areas, I get calls on the listening line from women who experience culture shock as they move from a city to a smaller town. Some communities are so small they feel they live in a fish bowl. If the pastor's wife joins an exercise class, everybody knows it. If they visit another church's Bible study, everybody knows it. They do not feel free to do things women normally do to reach out to other women.

The pastor's wife mold idea can be stifling too. Here in California I have a freedom to be who I am, to dress the way I desire, and to work out my schedule the way I want. But in many rural communities and older churches it is difficult for

**RISK FACTORS**

A recent survey of 228 pastors' wives revealed that 45% have no close friends within their churches, and almost half felt constrained in developing close friends in the local church context.

Duane Alleman, *Theology News and Notes,* Fuller Seminary

a pastor's wife to be herself. This adds up to isolation and makes it even more perplexing to live up to unrealistic expectations.

**Find a Friend**
**London/Wiseman**: Do you have any solutions to suggest? It seems many pastors' wives we know just live a life of quiet desperation.

**Riley**: One thing every pastor's wife must do is to find a close friend, even if it's just a pen pal. Friendship is a basic human survival need. So I suggest they go to a community service organization and volunteer. Try the library, the pregnancy counseling center, or anywhere they can expect to meet other Christian women with whom they can form close bonds.

**London/Wiseman**: What can the pastor do to help?

**Riley**: He needs to be willing to help with the children while she pursues friendship and other interests. He has had plenty of social interaction all week through his ministry, so he may want to stay home in the evening and relax. But he needs to consider her social needs, especially if she has been home all day with young children. He can help her by pursuing friendships with other couples and taking the time with her to get to know others on a social level.

**London/Wiseman:** What else can she do?

**Riley:** One of the best things a pastor's wife can do is to join or form a pastors' wives support group where wives get together, anywhere from every other week to every other month. The program can vary—sometimes it can be topic-oriented, sometimes simply a sharing of prayer requests, or sometimes just to get to know each other. The important thing is to have a setting where they can feel free to voice frustrations about ministry. We offer a good resource specially for developing such a group.

## When Parishioners Criticize
**London/Wiseman:** Do you often hear from pastors' wives who see their husbands being under savage attacks of criticism? What do those poor women do?

**Riley:** Amazingly, they are sometimes asked to take sides against their husbands. Occasionally people complain to them about their spouse. I often wonder if the church people expect a wife is going to say, "Yeah, you're right. My husband didn't handle that very well."

Sometimes people try to catch wives in the middle or send a message to the pastor they are afraid to say themselves. Of course, it is important that wives be wary and use a certain amount of discretion in the church. It can be tough.

**London/Wiseman:** What advice do you give them?

**Riley:** I advise them to gain an understanding of why people behave the way they do so they can be patient, understanding, and kind and not take these things personally. I'd just emphasize that gentle assertiveness can prevent it from recurring. Keep saying, "Have you made an effort to speak to my husband about this?" Or, "I'm sorry, but it would not be appropriate for me to bring this up to my husband when you are the one who is concerned."

**London/Wiseman:** Is it ever necessary to be confrontational?

**Riley:** Yes, I also believe in confrontation when it is necessary. Thus, when people complain, I send them back to the person they criticize and ask them to behave in a scriptural way about how disputes are to be resolved.

But it is a big issue. We hear on the listening line from many wives who cannot take the constant nitpicking about their husbands, themselves, the music program, or their children. Like everyone else, wives get fed up from years of little things.

## Protect the Children
**London/Wiseman:** What about the children?

**Riley:** Our listening line shows pastors' wives are extremely concerned about their children being exposed to problems in the church. They worry about the possibility of their leaving the faith at a later date because they saw their parents mistreated. Teenagers are most affected by church contention. Often they think things through and observe everything carefully.

As a preventative measure, I have tried to teach my children the difference between the perfection of Jesus and the imperfection of His people. We also try to help our children understand that people bring their personal problems to church with them. That means that when somebody says something cranky to Mommy, it has nothing to do with Mommy. It has to do with them.

**London/Wiseman:** Give an example of how you apply that idea.

**Riley:** Recently, I had an incident involving my thirteen-year-old daughter who works as an assistant in the church nursery. On a couple of occasions, a woman gave her petty complaints. When it happened with this same woman a third time, I decided to be confrontational in a firm but friendly way. So in case there was some sort of a blow-up, I waited after a church service until almost everyone had gone, and I spoke to this woman in private. That proved fruitful. I came on gently, but I do not think it will happen again with that lady.

**London/Wiseman:** How does this impact children on a long-term basis?

**Riley:** I think children appreciate being "protected" from unfair criticism and unfair demands made just because of their position. Also, the number one way to prevent cynicism and disillusionment and bitterness in growing PKs is to keep our own hearts and attitudes pure and free from bitterness which, as the Word says, "defiles many." If our children can see that we love Jesus and keep loving His people no matter what, they will become loving, forgiving disciples as well.

## If the Church Becomes a "Mistress"
**London/Wiseman:** What about when the pastor allows the church to become his "mistress," so the wife is left to spend endless days and nights alone while he tends the flock? What do you hear about this issue?

**Riley:** That is a really difficult question because the wife generally has been trying to talk to her husband about it. And those kind of husbands — church-first, workaholic types — find it difficult to really listen. I tell wives to keep at it. I suggest they choose a time when the husband is undistracted and say, "Look, this is what I'm going through. It's a lot more serious than you think. And I don't know what's going to happen if this doesn't stop."

I wish those pastors would take a hard look at their priorities. I'm sure they have not thought about the results of continually putting the church far above their family.

It's serious business. In our own community, a pastor's wife committed suicide last year. There have been three divorces among pastors in our geographic area within the last three months. And I know a pastor's wife across town who

**144**

blew straight out of the pressure cooker; she left her husband, the church, and even her children.

Family relationships have to be nurtured. It is as important as paying the bills or serving nourishing food to the family.

**London/Wiseman:** What if the husband does not listen?

**Riley:** I suggest that if the husband will not listen, then she bring somebody else in it. This has to be done skillfully. She could bring his denominational overseer or perhaps somebody she trusts on the board of elders. Just keep at it until he hears. It is better to do something fairly drastic to make him hear before she has a nervous breakdown, he has to hospitalize her, or she leaves.

**London/Wiseman:** He will hear her when he loses his ministry because of inattention to the marriage. Is there some way to bring the children into a higher level of significance?

**Riley:** We have a wonderful father-children tradition at our house. My husband reserves some time every Saturday as "Daddy Day" when he takes the kids out for half a day, usually in the morning. Then he spends the rest of the day putting the final touches on his sermon.

Jay does a wonderful job of modeling family relationships from the pulpit when he talks about Steve's baseball game and the plays our kids are doing at school. It is obvious from his references in the pulpit to family that he has significant involvement with his children. Everyone gains from this approach — our family, our marriage, and the church. Modeling the importance of family life helps church members respect your family time and not intrude unnecessarily.

There are many simple techniques. We have a telephone answering machine we use, especially at mealtime. We have date nights. We have lots of inspirational and preventative emphasis on marriage and family in the church too.

I especially remember one pastor's wife who called on the listening line; her husband was physically abusive to her and did not hear anything she said about improving the marriage.

Her husband/pastor had not given teaching, preaching, film series, or seminars on the family in their church because he did not want to hear it himself.

## When Wives Lose Respect

**London/Wiseman:** It's hard to imagine a pastor doing his work these days without a high emphasis on the Christian family. But that brings another concern to mind. Many pastors say that when they have misunderstandings with their wives, Satan lets that run over to Sunday morning. They have a disagreement just as they walk out the door for church, with no time to discuss it or settle it. Then the pastor has to face the responsibilities of the day with all that garbage inside him.

**Riley:** I know exactly what you are talking about.

**London/Wiseman:** With some pastors, that happens so often their wives are even disrespectful in the church. A recent letter from a pastor's wife states: "I've totally lost respect for my husband, so when I go to church I sit on the back pew and I knit." Now can you imagine what it must be like for that pastor to stand up to preach, knowing the disdain his wife holds for him at that moment? And can you image what that situation does to her spiritual life? What can they do?

**Riley:** This is an example of an extremely dysfunctional marriage where issues have been allowed to ferment instead of being addressed. This couple needs intensive counseling to be able to communicate, preferably with someone who understands and specializes in clergy issues.

**London/Wiseman:** What about professional counseling?

**Riley:** Jay and I have been married for nineteen years and had only been to a counselor a couple of times to work through our church split. Then we could pay somebody to listen to us complain all we wanted.

But we have had an extra heavy load recently. In addition

to the routine demands of ministry, we have one young man in a hospital two hours away getting a lung transplant, we have a former member and close friend two hours away in a different direction dying of breast cancer, we have people going through mid-life crises, and we have people who are unemployed.

As a result, I noticed my husband was getting depressed, so I urged him to go away for a two-week vacation at his brother's house. When he came back, he was just as depressed and tired as when he went. So I thought this was not a good situation, plus some unresolved disagreements were cropping up in our marriage that we were not talking through. He was depressed, overwhelmed, and taking on other people's problems as if they were his.

So I gently suggested counseling, and he agreed. We found a counselor who specializes in clergy issues. That is important, or else you end up being sort of a case study to educate the counselor about what is different about a clergy family. We are still in the process, and it is helping his ministry and our marriage. We have moved from issues which caused the depression into other things that we want to fine tune. Even healthy marriages can use a little fine tuning to prevent blowups in the future. It is the best thing we ever did for ourselves.

## Satisfactions in Shared Ministry

**London/Wiseman:** We have one other bomb to drop. A recent study shows that a high percentage of those surveyed thought the ministry had been a negative thing for their family. As you look at your four children and your husband, can you say that ministry has been something that you would do over again?

**Riley:** My first reaction is to start with God's will for your life. It would be miserable to be called to something and not do it. Being in the center of God's will is a comfortable place of fulfillment.

**London/Wiseman:** In reality, when we accepted the call of God into ministry, we signed on for the pain as well as the blessing.

**Riley:** That's right. I have met some older couples who have been in ministry maybe forty years, and they really do not know what I'm talking about when I discuss serious conflicts and troubles in the churches. There are a few couples in ministry who have led charmed lives: their congregations give them beautiful gifts every Christmas, they get thank-you notes all the time, and it's been wonderful. And, of course, life is rewarding in ministry when you see fruit. But it is conflict, forced terminations, serious discord, facing a contentious board, and having people mistreat your children — those big crises and small problems that make ministry tough.

**London/Wiseman:** We have talked about heavy things pertaining to the pastor's family, but what about the wonderful dimensions of being a pastor's wife?

**Riley:** There are many positives. High on my list is my love for my husband's flexible schedule. Though he is busy, his schedule is generally flexible. He can usually shift his work so he is available to go to the kids' parent-teacher meetings or to come home and have lunch with me once in awhile. With a little foresight and planning, he can usually be available for the kids when they get home from school or when I have some kind of meeting. Most men in other occupations just do not have flexible options in their work.

It is also special for me to have a partnership with Jay in his work. I am not an unofficial assistant pastor, but I do have a lot of influence in the church through him. Some of my creative ideas take root and are put into practice in the church. I'll tell you a funny thing about sharing our ideas. In the top drawer of Jay's desk at church, I keep a little booklet which I have titled "Jay's Great Ideas." But inside that notebook, I write my creative suggestions instead of nagging him about them, and then occasionally he goes through this book and says, "Hey! there's an idea I didn't think of." Many ministers' wives have not thought about this satisfying experience of having a special influence to help the church succeed.

Then there is the extended church family. My children are really nurtured by people in the church where they have so many aunt and uncle figures. There is also the way people look after our children — all of them have beautiful wardrobes that I have not purchased. People give them lovely clothing, and my children have never called them hand-me-downs. Each child is dressed far better than we could afford to purchase for them even if Jay had another vocation.

One also has to think about the exposure to interesting, godly people. Our children get much more exposure to guest speakers and visiting missionaries than other members of the church. Our family finds that exciting. As a matter of fact, my eleven-year-old says she is going to be a missionary because of this influence.

Together in ministry is a wonderful life if we work at it.

## Maximize Personal Growth in Your Marriage
Who will read this chapter first — the pastor or his wife? The pastor/husband might read first, looking for fresh ways to understand his wife's view of his commitment to his work. Or the wife might be the first to pick up the book to see if help is offered her. Either way, it is essential for the growth of a clergy marriage that both partners discuss these concepts and then design definite strategies for enriching their relationship.

These guidelines provide growth points for those who want to make a good marriage better. Then too these exercises offer life-changing guidance for those who feel trapped in a colorless, monotonous marriage relationship.

● *Connect with a Support Person*
Find a support person who cherishes your uniqueness and understands ministry — a soul friend to keep you focused on the meaning of ministry and remind you of its possible fulfillments.

You might consider someone raised in a pastor's home, a pastor's spouse, or a key layperson. Veteran ministers or their spouses, especially cheerful people who love kingdom work, might be who you need. Or you could consider pastoral retirees who are experienced at establishing priorities and dealing with pressures of ministry.

Try to find someone of your gender with spiritual stamina and emotional resilience. They also need a healthy relationship with God, a stable self-regard, a willingness to listen, and an ability to question self-imposed myths you have about ministry. The goals for this connection are dialogue, hope, prayer, and accountability.

● *Seek Both Solutions and Satisfactions*
Nearly everyone has enough problems to make them want to get off our whirling planet. One pastor's spouse angrily announced, "Of course I am an impossibility thinker. The church and my husband made me that way!" Perhaps most pastors easily identify with a minister who remarked, "I plan to have a serious burnout as soon as my schedule allows because I earned it."

Everyone knows many pastoral assignments are filled with threatening land mines waiting to explode in the minister's marriage. Nonetheless, simply highlighting the hardships leads nowhere. Surely, more can be done than criticizing the profession or describing the hazards.

Why not face down the fears and overpower the obstacles? And why not admit many marriage aggravations are human problems and not distinct ministry issues? Maybe the time has come to relinquish baseless biases about clergy marriages.

As a goliath forward step, bring your marriage apprehensions to some rational examination so you can appraise them accurately. Next, initiate a candid discussion of your concerns with your spouse. This strategy will move you both from overly generalized feelings of malaise about your marriage to identifiable issues you and your spouse can talk through and conceivably resolve.

● *Deprofessionalize Your Faith*

Christianity supplies satisfying nourishment for healthy marriages. However, it is frighteningly easy for anyone who lives close to the day-by-day events of the church to professionalize personal faith. It is also easy to depreciate or even bypass the spiritual disciplines because they sound so familiar. Clergy marriages often wither as a result.

Like everyone else, clergy couples need to feed their faith to make life happy and holy. The Father's nutritious provisions are lavish and convenient: assorted prayer forms like adoration, confession, thanks, petition and intercession; scriptural saturation that takes the Bible into the details of life; fasting that illuminates motives and intensifies dependence on God; spiritual formation calisthenics; celebration of creation; inspiration of church music; plus awareness of supernatural enablement to make ministry authentic and beautiful.

To enrich your marriage, strengthen your personal spiritual development in every possible way. Then share your discoveries with your spouse because such growth interaction will take Christ into the fabric of your marriage.

● *Construct a Christ-quality Marriage*

If homemade faith makes every human relationship better, then clergy marriages offer enormous potential for lifelong satisfaction to the couple. At the same time, a strong marriage provides a noble pattern for the congregation and community—it may be the only fulfilling marriage some dysfunctional people ever see. All that adds up to an impressive combination—individual contentment and laudable modeling for others.

How is such a marriage accomplished? A Christ-quality marriage starts with less emphasis on having one's own way. It requires refocusing from me to us. And it requires an expanded caring for each other. But a genuinely Christ-quality marriage offers the brimming pleasures of time-tested satisfactions which are rooted in fidelity, chastity, honor, truth, integrity, trust, respect, and purity.

**151**

- *Surrender Resistance to Ministry*

Some clergy couples live in a continuous state of agonizing anguish, believing God messed them up by putting them into the ministry. They feel victimized because they believe circumstances beyond their control have locked them into a gloomy existence.

But step closer to the facts. Living in a clergy marriage will never be as bad as some people expect nor as good as some wish it were. This reality is true of all marriages, regardless of the partner's occupation.

Authentic living in a satisfying clergy marriage demands relinquishment of all pent-up resistance to ministry. Resisting ministry hurts everyone. But there is a safe place in God's grace where resistance is seen as enslaving futility and acceptance becomes a liberating way of life.

We have a friend whose wife planted a church when she was fifty-nine years old. She studied to be ordained after her six children were grown at about the time her husband retired from long years of service as a postman. When a newspaper reporter asked the husband about this strange set of circumstances, he replied, "God can do what He wants. I want to wholeheartedly cooperate with His plan." His answer is exactly right for every ministry couple—wholehearted cooperation with God's plan. Give up resistance and discover joy in the journey.

- *Accept Love from the Congregation*

Helper types like pastors frequently have difficulty accepting love from those they serve. But every congregation has people who want to love their minister and his spouse. And the pastor is always more healthy for having received it.

Since love is contagious, it can be a two-way sharing between congregation and clergy couple. A wise Christian statesman commented, "As laypeople, we only grow as our pastor gives us love and he receives ours." Rejoice in this renewing reality—the Lord readily reveals Himself in the love of the people we serve.

● *Refuse to Abuse*

Many moderns do not know what to think about society's broadened concept of abuse. But if abuse actually means emotional or spiritual mistreatment, then it may be epidemic in many clergy marriages. Its many destructive expressions include biting sarcasm, passive dissension, trivial pouting, and emotional estrangement.

Any pastor can abuse his marriage by giving so much of himself to the church that he has no energy left for the most important people in his life. Flying under the motive of giving first priority to the church, a pastor can easily neglect and harm his family.

Abuse flows the other way when the pastor's spouse resents the church and feels deserted by her husband. Then she criticizes his parenting, nags about his long hours, and belittles the congregation. Then the walls of isolation go up even higher.

When that happens, husband and wife exist in lonely, emotional isolation. Though they may never divorce, they live in two disconnected, miserable worlds. Though they eat at the same table, sleep in the same bed, and view the same TV programs, they are worlds apart—separated, neglected, and frustrated.

Such slavery can be broken when either marriage partner takes the spirit of Christ into the marriage. Then, both partners will have room to grow as forgiveness, reconciliation, and tenderness replace nagging, criticizing, and rigidity.

● *Guard Against Perils*

Good marriages require rigorous effort. It is especially true for a clergy couple because personal wholeness is such a necessary component in the life of the authentic pastor. But because of built-in demands, a clergy couple's sound marriage requires more effort on both partner's part.

Hear the anguish of a pastor suffering from moral collapse: "My wife and I failed each other. We indifferently starved each other emotionally until our marriage died a natural death from neglect." Perils like that can be escaped if the pastor and spouse work to be best friends and to be life's greatest pleasures for each other.

Like time out in a basketball game, marriage tensions need instant attention. Always play up the pluses and play down the demands ministry makes on marriage.

Emotional isolation can be avoided by creating a weekly time island of spiritual, emotional, and physical intimacy where you can be alone together to catch up on all dimensions of your marriage. Stand firm against every titillating temptation. Remove yourself from any circumstance that even faintly compromises your commitments to each other or diminishes the influence of your combined service for Christ. Extraordinary ability is not required. It only takes plain old hard work coupled with a willingness to resist every trace of seduction.

## THE CONTEMPORARY CHALLENGE
### HIGHLIGHT ADVANTAGES

Cherish and emphasize the privileges you enjoy in a clergy marriage. In the interview, Linda Riley underscores an impressive list of advantages such as flexible time, unique opportunities to impact peoples' lives, and extended family in the church, special people who visit the pastor's home, and the opportunity to share in shaping the church's future ministry.

Talk up the advantages built into your marriage. Try listing your specific benefits. For too long, clergy couples have emphasized what they miss by being in ministry. One pastor even made the foolish mistake of saying from his pulpit, "If I had not gone into the ministry, I could have been president of General Motors by now." One wag replied in a stage whisper that could be heard for at least three pews, "Yes, and you might have been a garbage collector by now too."

It is time to count the blessings pastoral ministry provides. After counting them, it would be helpful to say to each other, to the children, and to ourselves, "This is a good way to live and we are blessed by the benefits."

---

**RENEWAL STRATEGIES**
**MAKE YOUR WIFE GLAD SHE MARRIED A PASTOR**

✔ *Connect with a Support Person*
✔ *Seek Both Solutions and Satisfactions*
✔ *Deprofessionalize Your Faith*
✔ *Construct a Christ-quality Marriage*
✔ *Surrender Resistance to Ministry*
✔ *Accept Love from the Congregation*
✔ *Refuse to Abuse*
✔ *Guard Against Perils*

---

# PART
## THREE

# Renewing
# the Pastor

# EIGHT

# Recovery from Stress and Burnout

"I find it difficult to get motivated to do pastoral calling or personal evangelism. I'm having lots of doubts regarding my calling and about my faith as well." — a pastor from California

While no pastor goes seeking stress or burnout, it often comes with the territory. What a minister does, the hours he keeps, and the raw side of human nature keep him constantly exposed to the possibilities of stress and burnout. Since he is at risk every day, he must continually apply preventative measures to his inner world to keep himself spiritually and emotionally well. And should the malady strike, he must recognize and treat the first symptoms. If he suffers a full-blown attack, he must use all the remedies of faith and emotional health he so often prescribes for persons in the parish.

Though the contemporary pastor may not be able to avoid his own tensions, pressures, and anxieties, he can choose his responses. And though he cannot minister without in-depth relationships with persons who feel tortured by a hundred kinds of brokenness, he can use the experiences of others in their broken places to expand his own soul.

Study helps for prevention, diagnosis, prescription, and res-

157

toration are suggested in the following interview with
Archibald Hart, who is Professor of Psychology and Dean of
the Graduate School of Psychology at Fuller Seminary.

## Interview with Archibald Hart

**London/Wiseman**: Dr. Hart, you have been leading a crusade
to help pastors understand, prevent, and recover from burnout. Let's start with your enlightening idea of the basic relationship between adrenalin and stress.

**Hart**: Post-adrenalin depression seems to be the most descrip-
tive term I have found. Nearly everyone seems to have some
firsthand experience of this physical condition following an
unusual heavy demand on the human system. A pastor
should expect it on Monday after a demanding Sunday when
he has had a long, continuous, heavy adrenalin drain.

**London/Wiseman**: Is that the same as Monday morning
gloom?

**Hart**: Exactly. The same kind of drain happens to pastors, to
speakers, to athletes, to salesmen, to politicians, to doctors
after they have charged themselves up for a big event. Then
after doing their best, they have a significant letdown — a discomforting depression. That makes Monday tough for pastors.

**London/Wiseman**: What causes those depressed feelings?

**Hart**: It's an aftermath of being too revved up, biologically
speaking, over the weekend. Lots of adrenalin is required for
much of ministry. Consider preaching, for example. If you are
going to keep people awake, you better have lots of energy
going.

**London/Wiseman**: Then you think it is a physical problem
rather than an emotional or spiritual problem?

**Hart**: It's simply an overuse of the system of energy that suddenly crashes on Monday morning and puts the body into

short-term depression. It's the body saying, "I need to rest. I need to recover. I need time for rejuvenation."

**London/Wiseman:** If it's physical, why do so many pastors whip themselves like it is a spiritual problem?

**Hart:** I wish I knew. I guess that is the reason I'm on this soapbox to free pastors from guilt over a natural situation. They mistakenly see it as spiritual — that Satan is getting me, and my ministry was not good yesterday. But mostly, it is simply a lack of understanding of adrenalin management.

**London/Wiseman:** Or maybe a gift from God calling us to replenish, to slow down, and to regroup.

**Hart:** That's it. I really think this system is designed as part of God's intelligent creation to facilitate the healing process within our bodies. And if we scorn that process, we do so to our own peril because the consequences of ignoring those calls by the body for rejuvenation will invariably be an increased proneness to burnout and stress.

## Monday — A Bad Day Off
**London/Wiseman:** Let's share a scenario from our own pastoral practice. We often did not take Monday off because we wanted to face the music at the beginning of the week. That way we worked through those Monday morning glooms by about noon, and then we could have a week ahead — ready to go. Does that fit in with your idea?

**Hart:** I think you have something there, providing you did not go full speed on Monday.

**London/Wiseman:** Should the activity be low demand?

**Hart:** I advise pastors to use Monday to do low-level energy or routine activities. That is the time to tidy your desk, throw out the trash or do some filing. I worry about your terms "facing the music" and "getting ready to go." If you mean low exertion activities, I am for it.

**London/Wiseman:** What should be avoided?

**Hart:** It's not a time to pick a fight, go hassle those who annoy you, make a critical decision, or deal with difficult budget problems. If you get your adrenalin up again, you may feel all right, but you have robbed your body of rest and recuperation.

**London/Wiseman:** What does that say to thousands of pastors who traditionally take Monday off?

**Hart:** Monday is a bad idea for a day off. I recommend a day off later in the week—maybe Thursday or Friday—when energy is good, you feel alive, and you can give your family quality time for bonding and recreation.

**London/Wiseman:** That idea could greatly improve family relationships. Many pastors faithfully take Monday off, thinking they are doing a good thing for themselves and their family. In fact, too often pastors cannot give their families all of themselves on Monday because they are too preoccupied with the weekend at the church.

**Hart:** Many pastors' wives tell me they get out of the house on Monday. They say, "I split. I do not want to be around him."

**London/Wiseman:** What are the symptoms in this heavy adrenalin draw?

**Hart:** You are irritable. You have little patience. You want to be quiet. You do not want to talk. You do not want to be with anybody. You are not good at communication.

**London/Wiseman:** What a list! And what a bad deal for the pastor's wife who only gets time from her husband on Monday.

**Hart:** Exactly! That is exactly what scores of pastors give their spouses on Monday. And that is the only time they give their wives. It is not quality time, and it is not adequate to build a good marriage.

**London/Wiseman:** Then you think a clear correlation exists between Monday morning doldrums and troubled pastors' marriages?

**Hart:** I am afraid so.

**London/Wiseman:** Is it worse among those who take ministry very seriously?

**Hart:** Yes, of course. It seems that our evangelical world is adrenally dependent and driven. We are committed, as we should be, to the Great Commission. Obviously, that means lots of work for most of us. But somehow we have lost sight of the importance of being able to rest in Christ. Christ is our Sabbath rest, and we must learn not to usurp His work—only to be a servant to it.

## Distinctions between Stress and Burnout

**London/Wiseman:** That leads naturally to our next question. Is there a difference between stress and burnout?

**Hart:** Yes, they are two different conditions and experiences. Unfortunately, most of the literature has not made an adequate differentiation between stress and burnout.

**London/Wiseman:** Begin with stress.

**Hart:** Stress is primarily a biological phenomenon: too much adrenalin and too much pressure. You are on high and using too much energy to perform certain functions. You have too many deadlines. And you are often overcommitted. Stress is the loss of fuel and energy which often produces panic, phobic, and anxiety-type disorders.

**London/Wiseman:** Sounds like an average day in the life of Pastor Joe Faithful. What happens in the human body?

**Hart:** The body is in an emergency mode so cholesterol goes up, blood pressure goes up, the heartbeat goes up, and hands get colder. It is accelerated wear and tear on the body which leads to stomach ulcers or gives you high blood pressure. It may clog your arteries and put you on the road to heart disease. That is stress.

The stressed individual is characterized by over-engagement and the emotions become overreactive. Stress may kill you prematurely, and then you will not have enough time to finish what you started.

**London/Wiseman**: It sounds like the worst kind of self-imposed cruelty.

**Hart**: It is.

**London/Wiseman**: How is stress different from burnout?

**Hart**: Burnout is much more of an emotional response.

**London/Wiseman**: What are its characteristics?

**Hart**: In burnout, the victim becomes demoralized and knows things are not going right. People are not affirming him. He begins to lose the vision. He suffers from loss of hope. Burnout often results in a disengagement from the main task. It often has symptoms of depersonalization and detachment. And a state of crushing discouragement—almost despair—sets in. Demoralization is a good way to summarize it.

**London/Wiseman**: Many pastors live with feelings of helplessness and hopelessness every day. Some live that way all their lives.

**Hart**: It's tough—very difficult. Think of the misery for the sufferer: I no longer care. I no longer feel like I once did. My horizons are closing in. My heart is numb. It's difficult to love anymore.

**London/Wiseman**: Think of the woman who stands by his side and the kids. The pastor comes to a place where he almost doesn't care anymore.

**Hart**: Right! He does get to the place where he says, "I do not care." In the pastorate, this process often comes about when the victim has no adequate emotional support, no one to talk with — when he is isolated, alone, or even cut off from people who could help. Then he turns inward because he thinks he has to be strong and not share his problems with anyone else. That's burnout.

**London/Wiseman:** Where does it lead?

**Hart:** Stress and burnout both lead to the same place — depression. Stress and burnout just take you there by different routes.

## Four A's: Arrogance, Addiction, Aloneness, Adultery

**London/Wiseman:** Do stress and burnout lead a person to erratic behavior such as has been chronicled in the newspaper regarding highly visible religious leaders?

**Hart:** Yes, they do. A Harvard Medical School specialist has identified four A's in the secular world that I think I see at work in the Christian world.

**London/Wiseman:** Four A's? What do you mean?

**Hart:** The first is *arrogance* where the person says I can make it and I can do it myself; I do not need anyone else. And that person begins to make his own rules.

**London/Wiseman:** That's fairly common among pastors who are in trouble.

**Hart:** The second is an adventurous *addiction* where you become so taken up, so excited, so energized by what you are doing.

**London/Wiseman:** Many ministers have that tendency too.

**Hart:** The third is *aloneness*. That is the point where you are at risk with depression because you cut yourself off from other people.

And the fourth is *adultery* where individuals begin to see sex as the only thing that can give a real kick. They turn to sex to make up for the sense of loss in their lives.

**London/Wiseman:** What a devastating downward process! How can it happen to pastors who live so close to holy things?

**Hart:** I believe those four A's are as much a risk for pastors as for anyone in the secular world striving for success at something. These are consequences of too much stress and burnout.

**London/Wiseman:** But shouldn't things be different for pastors?

**Hart:** Ultimately, it is a spiritual problem. It has to do with not keeping a balanced spiritual orientation in your ministry.

**Type A and B Personality**
**London/Wiseman:** As you describe the four A's, it seems that they partially describe the type A personality.

**Hart:** Isn't that amazing?

**London/Wiseman:** And frightening!

**Hart:** It's amazing that the A-type individual is the one prone to being arrogant, and he is likely to suffer stress while the B-type person is more typically the pastor who experiences burnout.

**London/Wiseman:** Nearly everyone is acquainted with A-type, but what is a B-type personality?

**Hart:** B-type people usually do not rush around like you and me. They are more reflective and feel things more deeply. Loss for them is a much more painful thing. They are more introverted, and they do not share their pains and their hurts with others. So they begin to feel demoralization much more quickly, which leads to burnout.

**London/Wiseman:** So A-types are more prone to stress and B-types are more inclined to burnout?

**Hart**: Yes.

## Warnings of Stress and Burnout
**London/Wiseman**: What are the red flags that lead to either stress or burnout? What signals a pastor that he is on a collision course with either one?

**Hart**: The symptoms are these—and I am confessing because I am A-type. It's a denial that you are addicted to a high, to excitement, to new challenges, to new projects. You do not like doing the old routine stuff. You do not like maintenance. You like planning new projects.

So the first thing is to admit that you are high risk and to face up to your symptoms. Are you getting sick often, which may be a sign that you're compromising your immune system. Stomach problems, ulcers, headaches—any of the classic stress symptoms that come regularly—must be taken as a sign that you are pushing yourself too fast, too hard, and you are overstressed.

**London/Wiseman**: What about the burnout question?

**Hart**: The signs are much more subtle. Slowly you find yourself beginning to hate the telephone. You begin to avoid people. You go into a panic whenever there is a new problem. You begin to lose confidence in yourself. And you often become narrowly focused on petty issues.

**London/Wiseman**: Can you illustrate?

**Hart**: Yes, I have a graphic illustration. One pastor in advanced stages of burnout would go to his office on the second floor of the church building, overlooking the parking lot which is next to a supermarket. He would sit there for hours looking out the window to see if he could catch people parking in the church lot and going to the supermarket. Keep in mind that the church is not having services and has no need for the parking spaces. Then when someone dared to park on church property, he would run down the stairs and angrily tell them to move their car. See how petty it is. We call it the fetishization of tasks.

**London/Wiseman**: Then probably a great deal of paranoia sets in as well.

**Hart**: Yes, and you become suspicious. Everyone is out to get you. And why did they say that in the committee meeting? Those are signs that one is losing perspective and balance — burned out.

## RISK FACTORS

Long-term stress, according to the Alban Institute, is no stranger to American pastors. An estimated 20% of the nation's 300,000 clergy suffer from it. One recent year when the Southern Baptist Convention paid out $64 million in medical claims benefits for pastors' claims, stress-related illnesses were second in dollar amount only to maternity benefits.

*Current Thoughts & Trends,*
December 1992

**London/Wiseman**: Why do we feel like our lives are passing before us while you talk?

**Hart**: All of us have some of these characteristics because we have this great urgency to go save the world before the year 2000.

**London/Wiseman**: We are highly motivated but find ourselves depleted of energy. We find ourselves being human and oftentimes not very spiritual. Then our spouses walk through the living room, or sit on the couch beside us, or sit in the congregation in front of us, listening to someone they do not even know anymore. What do we say to them?

### Building a Support System
**Hart**: In my opinion, when facing stress or burnout, we have to resist overloading the family system for a solution. Most marriages simply cannot take these pressures. I think a pastor needs to have a support system outside the family. Then when he goes back to the family, he is not solely dependent on them to provide him with emotional sustenance, spiritual support, and needed healing. It is important that the family have some idea of what is going on, but they should not be expected to be the sole support of a husband/father in difficulty.

**London/Wiseman:** What do pastors' wives tell you about this issue?

**Hart:** They tell me, "He dumps on me. I dread the moment he comes through the door because I know what is going to happen. He does not want to listen to my problems. He does not want to hear about the kids—either good or bad. He thinks all of that is petty stuff. So I have to sit there and receive all that dumping." It's inhumane.

**London/Wiseman:** Where can the pastor get the support he needs?

**Hart:** He needs to build an adequate support system, preferably with peers—persons to whom he can turn for nurture, to share his hurt, to open his soul, and to unburden himself. It is in such bearing of one another's burdens that one finds the healing that Christ can bring.

**London/Wiseman:** Before we close, tell us about the books you have written dealing with these issues.

**Hart:** The book I wrote most for myself was *Adrenalin and Stress*. My wife says I wrote that book because she prayed for me. It chronicles my personal battle with stress. I had lots of unfinished business from childhood that I carried over into adulthood. And that is true for many pastors. It will be even more true in the future as more people come into the ministry from dysfunctional families.

Pastors also need to deal with the unfinished business of having a bad experience in one church, then moving on to another church, and then to the church after that. There is often lots of unfinished pain in those transitions.

**London/Wiseman:** And did you write a book dealing with divorce?

**Hart:** Yes, the title is *Healing Adult Children of Divorce*. That book is my own recovery from the painful damage when my parents divorced when I was twelve.

**London/Wiseman:** Both of those books sound like they have been therapeutic for you.

**Hart:** That's absolutely right. I think many of us write for ourselves, and other people simply read over our shoulders.

## Every Man Must Learn to Live with His Profession

Archibald Hart helps us see that pace and balance are needed for the pastor's spiritual and emotional health. A useful way to start is to consider the solid insight his father-in-law physician gave John A. Sanford, "Every man must learn to live with his profession."[1] In his book *Ministry Burnout*, Sanford develops this idea when he advises a pastor to think of his work as that of a long-distance runner who cannot overspend himself by running the first part of the race at a pace he cannot maintain.[2]

Everyone knows modern ministry has more demands than pastors have ever known before. But it must be managed and balanced if the church is to have leadership and future society is to feel the strength of the Gospel. Maybe these are the best of times and the worst — best because we have to rethink so much, and worst because the changing demands are so rapid that we find them hard to respond to.

In protecting himself against burnout and stress, the pastor must seek to be his best self and to do his best work but never live with the burden of an artificial persona. Being something we are not takes too much energy. The burden to live up to sham dramatically increases stress. It is far more healthy for the pastor to try to live up to his absolutely true best self at all times. The people he leads will likely welcome such reality in their pastor; surely the Lord is pleased with the way He made us.

Why not embark on a lifelong pilgrimage of wholehearted adventure in the pastorate? It might make you good at avoiding stress and burnout. Here's a list of first steps to consider.

● *Rethink Your Day Off*
Monday may not be the best day off for you in light of Hart's adrenalin-draw idea. Perhaps you need to get a slow start into

your week and do light work that day. At least for one day per week, be one-half as good to yourself as you have been to your parishioners. One of the mystics advised, "Remember, you hold your body and nervous system in trust from God, and you must treat His property well." God approves of your taking care of His servant, and it is a good investment in your future.

This simple adjustment might provide colossal improvements in your family in a week or a month. Then everyone gains – spouse, children, church, and self.

● *Understand Your Personality Type*
Some pastors, because they see themselves in both types, will have difficulty sorting through the differences between A- and B-type personalities. The classification is not as important as it is to know whether you are more susceptible to stress or burnout. Then you can seek corrective action or help at the first sign of either. It helps to change your behavior, but often that will not be sufficient to prevent future problems. Better yet, prevent the root causes of tensions in your ministry.

● *Welcome Spouse into Prevention*
Often the pastor's wife sees possible solutions but does not offer them because she thinks they will be ignored or scorned. When you view marriage and family as an energy to enrich the whole of life, your time with them provides prevention, remedy, and enablement – something significantly different from viewing home relationships as another series of oppressive obligations.

● *Reach across Isolation*
Many pastors are actually isolated from their peers by geography or theology, so they have to intentionally reach across these boundaries for friendship and support. Others are loners by disposition. Either way, the isolation is real; it heightens stress and burnout. But successful ministers cannot be "lone rangers." They need one another. Groups of

pastors have much to learn from the support group movement that is sweeping the country.

● *Take Charge of Your Prevention or Recovery*
Just as no one else will get you to a doctor for pain in your side or a dentist for pain in your jaw, no one else is likely to take drastic steps in dealing with your burnout or stress. You alone control the action.

In an upbeat letter to H.B., a pastor outlines his bold remedial action for a less stressful future: "I have been battling this emotional stress for eight years and have finally decided to make some changes in my lifestyle and deal with it. Thus my letter to you. I will be undergoing a complete physical check-up next week, have begun a diet to lose some excess weight, and have recently begun a walking exercise three days a week. I am even trying to rotate my daily schedule. My next step is to seek counseling from a Christian agency which may help me as I contemplate a career change even at fifty-eight years of age."

● *Confront Your Addictions*
An addiction is any fixation of mind or body that commands so much attention that normal functioning is not possible and spiritual development is either neglected or nonexistent. It is a frightening idea to think that some pastors might use ministry as a narcotic to keep from developing personal relationships, especially in marriage and family.

Most of us in the helping professions think of addictions as having to do with drugs, tobacco, or alcohol. However, many pastors might also be helped to think through Hart's idea of addiction to a high—such as to excitement, challenge, or new projects. All of these happen often in the pastorate, but they are not the normal day-by-day operation of life, family, or ministry.

● *Limit Number of Clinging Vines*
Every church has at least one person—many have several—whom therapists describe as needing "maintenance counsel-

ing." These are people who do not have the emotional or spiritual energy to live life on their own. Some of them, perhaps, could go on their own strength, but for their own reasons they want to cling to you, the pastor. To the man who remained ill at Bethsaida's pool for thirty-eight years, Jesus spoke the startling sentence, "Get up, take your mat, and walk" (Mark 2:9). While many of these clinging individuals who come to you will never be strong or able to walk alone, the pastor cannot simply be bled to death emotionally by carrying too many of them at any one time. The danger: he may become like them. If the load is allowed to get too heavy, the pastor becomes stressed or burned out instead of the needy person becoming whole. Like a blood transfusion, the pastor can give only so much help before endangering himself.

● *Get Back to Doing What You Want to Do*
Could it be that much stress comes from dreading or even resisting some phase of ministry? Lloyd J. Ogilvie puts the idea in a positive light, "People do not burn out from doing too much of what they delight in doing."[3] Most pastors could use more satisfaction and less obligation.

It sounds strange to say that a pastor should do what he *wants* to do when there is so much that *has* to be done. But, the categories *urgent* and *essential* are difficult dimensions to sort out in ministry. The pastor must know the difference. By doing the essentials like preaching, teaching, and pastoral care, the pastor gets past the urgent pressing demands to the more satisfying achievements of impacting people in life-changing ways. Most pastors could use more satisfaction and less obligation.

## THE CONTEMPORARY CHALLENGE
### SEEK GOD'S GUIDANCE FOR BALANCE

Though it sounds mystical, it is still true that God guides surrendered wills and Christ-centered thinking. By close association with Him, with your peers, and with spiritually aware laypersons, you can find your way through the thicket of overloads. Most pastors cannot get by with doing a whole lot less, but they can ask the Father to help them balance their lives. No datebook, time management seminar, or pastoral strategy book can do the work for you. And it is doubtful that you can do it for yourselves, or you would have already done it.

We who preach guidance by the Lord can make full use of it for ourselves. Finding balance is the key to avoiding stress and burnout. Ogilvie helps us again, "I've never known a person to have a nervous breakdown doing what the Lord wills. He never asks us to do more than He is willing to provide strength for us to do. He does not guide us into burnout."[4]

## RENEWAL STRATEGIES
### PREVENTION FROM STRESS AND BURNOUT

- ✔ Rethink Your Day Off
- ✔ Understand Your Personality Type
- ✔ Welcome Spouse into Prevention
- ✔ Reach across Isolations
- ✔ Take Charge of Your Prevention
- ✔ Confront Your Addictions
- ✔ Limit Number of Clinging Vines
- ✔ Get Back to Doing What You Want to Do

**NINE**

# Pursue
# Personal Holiness

"I truly long to be a spiritual leader. I no longer want to be a
manager of a church or CEO of a nonprofit corporation." – from a
pastor in Tennessee

*P*oor pastor! Modern ministry has become such an
endless grind of crippling crises that many pastors
question why God did not stop them at the blooming
of their call or wonder why a seasoned pastoral veteran did
not slow them down on their hurried path to ordination.

*Blessed pastor!* Griffith's imaginary true-to-life words from
Jesus say it well: "So you feel beaten, bullied, and whipped by
the demands that people make on you, inconsiderate people
who are so troubled that they can think of no one but themselves. Well, that's what you bargained for when you entered
*my* ministry. And it is *my* ministry."

Griffith continues his digging around the roots of ministerial motivation: "Read about it in the Gospels. They tell you
about a typical day in *my* earthly career, a day that begins,
continues and ends with crises, a day of involvement in human need, battling with human hypocrisy, a day that leaves
*me* depleted, exhausted and ready to quit – except that I find
renewal in prayer."[1]

We respond with a high sounding excuse, "Though I am no better than my Lord, I do not have the resources for ministry He had." But we can have them.

These possibilities pull at our motives as we experience the dual challenges of the world and the persistent inner call to be holy. Both are needed. We know we want an active outer life resourced by a holy inner life. But how can we have both?

*Energized pastor!* God "resources" us even when ministry depletes us. God enables us when ministry baffles us. God makes us sufficient for every situation we encounter for Him. What exhilarating news—this inward pursuit of Christlikeness rejuvenates purpose, renews stamina, and rekindles passion.

The holy life pays off in the best kind of living as it shapes us into Christlikeness—even in our frustrations and at the close of demanding days. The supernatural reality that pastors so often forget is that in ministry our whole self is being molded into the image of God's Son even as we labor for Him.

## The Pursuit of Personal Holiness
Intimacy with Christ nourishes ministry and the pursuit of holiness keeps the soul in shape. On the contrary, when a pastor feels perplexed, strained, or fearful, his life tends to become shallow and his ministry perfunctory. While many ministry frustrations are external and environmental—even out of our own control—our only sure way to revitalize the church is to renew our own inner world in fresh old ways. That is the exciting journey Jerry Bridges helps us start.

## Interview with Jerry Bridges
London/Wiseman: Let's discuss personal holiness and its impact on ministry. The titles of your books suggest a personal pilgrimage: *The Pursuit of Holiness, The Practice of Godliness, Trusting God,* and now *Transforming Grace.* Are they?

Bridges: Yes, *The Practice of Godliness* is a sequel to *The Pursuit of Holiness,* which started when the lights went on for me that Ephesians tells us to put on the new man as well as put off the old man. *The Pursuit of Holiness* focuses largely on dealing with sin or putting off the old man. But an equal emphasis is needed for putting on the new man—those godly traits that Paul calls the fruit of the Spirit in Galatians 5.

**London/Wiseman:** That progression is so significant for pastors. It was a life-changing day in pastoral ministry when we realized that personal holiness was the most important thing we could bring to the congregation and to our families. A miraculous new chapter of ministry opened when we understood that pursuing personal holiness was the essential underpinning of ministry. Would you agree?

**Bridges:** Absolutely. I believe ministry flows out of our lives— out of who we really are. Therefore, we cannot adequately convey spiritual reality to others if we are not pursuing holiness. The people always pick up on our weakness and follow us into spiritual shallowness if we are not pursuing a holy character and a pure lifestyle.

**London/Wiseman:** Often we hear people describe a pastor as being godly. Now that does not mean he pastors the biggest church in the country. It really means he is a spiritually authentic person who causes others to believe he lives close to God. Our pursuit of holiness is amazingly attractive to the people we lead.

Now we firmly believe a pastor can be holy and successful at the same time. But if we have to choose, we want to be godly men.

**Bridges:** I agree, but a pastor can be both holy and effective. One could make a strong case that no pastor is effective who is not holy.

## Living Confidently in God's Unfailing Love
**London/Wiseman:** The message about holy living is clear in your book *Transforming Grace* and the subtitle—*Living Confidently in God's Unfailing Love*—amplifies the grace issue.

What is the main thesis of the book and where did it start?

**Bridges:** The book started while I was writing *The Pursuit of Holiness* fourteen years ago. The earlier book caused me to sharpen the focus on holiness in my own life so I was forced to question myself, "Am I really practicing what I am writing in this book?" In that process, I always came back to an awareness that anyone who seriously pursues holiness must come to grips with the grace of God. Without an emphasis on grace, we lapse into a performance relationship with God. Then our relationship with Him is gauged on how well we have been doing in pursuing holiness rather than depending on the provisions of Christ. This interdependence of grace and holiness made me consider titling the book *Saved by Grace but Living by Sweat.*

**London/Wiseman:** Thousands of pastors can relate to that concept.

**Bridges:** There is a fascinating reality in this relationship between grace and works. We all know we are saved by grace. Thus we agree with the biblical teaching and preach it. Then for some strange reason we lapse into living by the sweat of our performance in our day-to-day relationship with God. Then we think if I have been good today, I expect God to bless me. But I do not expect much from God if I have fallen on my face today.

**London/Wiseman:** In that vein, we assume we must be in tune with God if the church is succeeding, if our ministry is well-received, if attendance is growing, if people are being saved and being filled with the Spirit. It seems we think we are more personally spiritual when the pews are packed and everybody is saying nice things about us. We think all this success could not happen if we were not holy.

**Bridges:** It is easy to forget that visible success is not the issue, but genuine relationship with Christ and absolute dependence on Him. It is possible to be successful without being holy, or it is feasible to be a miserable failure without being holy.

**London/Wiseman:** That is exactly right. Tell us more about your discoveries about transforming grace and what it means to live confidently in God's unfailing love.

**Bridges:** The reality is that many believers do not fully enjoy living in God's grace so it has a transforming effect on their character. In 2 Corinthians 3:18, Paul says we are being transformed into His likeness from one degree of glory to another. In the context of 2 Corinthians 3, Paul is contrasting the glory of the Law which came through Moses with the exceedingly greater glory of the Gospel. So when Paul talks in this passage about the glory of Christ, he is really discussing the glory of Christ as we see it in the Gospel.

I believe we need to put ourselves up against the Gospel every day. By this frequent and intentional application of the Gospel, we build continual realization of God's grace and its transforming effect on our character. We need a review every day to see if we are living it. And when we do such a daily reassessment, we get excited about the Gospel at work in us and become so aware of the grace of God that we want to live an effective Christian life, and it continually transforms us.

## What Is Holiness?
**London/Wiseman:** In *Transforming Grace,* a whole chapter is devoted to describing holiness. In brief capsule form, what do you mean when you speak about holiness?

**Bridges:** I mean holiness is conformity to the likeness of Christ. Paul says in Romans 8:29 that we have been predestined to be conformed to the likeness of God's Son. The likeness of Christ is the bottom line of holiness for me.

**London/Wiseman:** What a challenging and satisfying possibility — conformity to the character of Christ.

**Bridges:** That means we must deal with sin in our lives. But we also put on godly character by continually dealing with the question, "How can I be like Christ, and how would He live in my circumstances?"

Jesus hates sin and loves holiness. The writer of Hebrews says in 1:9 that our Lord loved righteousness and He hated wickedness. That is what He wants us to do. We should hate wickedness; we should hate sin; we should resist sin; and we should put sin to death.

But there is much more—Jesus also loved righteousness. Consequently, we should love righteousness—that is living a godly character. That is what holiness is—hating sin and loving righteousness in the details of our lives.

**London/Wiseman**: Let us get beyond some possible theological difficulties and make personal holiness practical for ministers.

As pastors, it seemed when we were on a successful fast track, receiving accolades and commendations from parishioners and peers, that we were less holy than at any other time. Were we different from others?

**Bridges**: Success or lack of it is never a reliable way to measure personal holiness.

**London/Wiseman**: In seasons of success, we sometimes tried to paddle our own canoe. Perhaps there was too much pride, too much dependence on self, or not enough trust in God's transforming grace. But the effort was awfully human—paddling a canoe rather than moving ahead in the power of Christ. But hundreds of pastors are like that. They try to do ministry in their own strength without relying on God's transforming grace. It is a subtle but deadly temptation.

**Bridges**: That is so true.

**London/Wiseman**: What difference does it make if you had a great crowd and a big offering last Sunday if you find your own heart uninhabited and empty so you are not satisfied or fulfilled?

**Bridges**: One way to gauge ministry is to ask yourself, "If the

Holy Spirit were to back out of this effort, would it collapse?" Many ministries would continue because they are humanly produced programs.

Let me illustrate from my own assignment. I work in an administrative capacity with the Navigators where I deal with business and legal issues. But I am just as dependent on the Holy Spirit to enable me to function in this work as a pastor is in preaching or building a church. In my time alone with God I keep reminding myself of my dependence on Him.

God honors dependence on Him. Every morning in my quiet time, I read the Bible and pray, but I also take time to sit back and evaluate whether I am depending on the Holy Spirit or on my own talents and the fine staff around me.

**London/Wiseman:** Personal holiness requires time with God, doesn't it? Pastors, busy with their ministries, so often overlook that point.

We think of highly visible pastors and Christian leaders whose lives are filled to the brim. We do not know how they travel, speak, write, administrate, and still allow adequate time for the Lord to do for them and to them what you have just been discussing. Though details differ in every ministry, the pressures to bypass daily renewing are real for every pastor regardless of the size of his church.

Many pastors write saying, "My life is out of balance. I do not have time to pray. I do not have time for my family. I do not have time to fulfill the expectations of my church. I am going crazy."

> ### RISK FACTORS
>
> Peter Wagner surveyed 572 pastors across America to find out about their prayer lives. The results concerning actual prayer time follow:
> - the pastors spent an average of 22 minutes a day in prayer
> - 57% spend less than 20 minutes a day in prayer
> - 34% spend between 20 minutes and 1 hour a day in prayer
> - 9% pray for an hour or longer daily
>
> *Ministries Today,* Nov/Dec 1992

All of that adds up to the strong possibility they are probably not spending much time with the Lord either.

**Bridges:** Personal time with God is usually the first thing that goes in our busyness.

**London/Wiseman:** Listen to a quote from your book *Transforming Grace:* "My observation of Christendom is that most of us tend to base our personal relationship with God on our performance instead of His grace. If we've performed well, whatever well is in our opinion, then we expect God to bless us. If we haven't done well, our expectations are reduced accordingly. In that sense, we live by works rather than by grace. We are saved by grace. We are living by the sweat of our performance."

That's a superb summation of the situation. Are clergy more prone to performance mentality than their parishioners?

**Bridges:** I think more. Most of the correspondence I receive about *Transforming Grace* comes from pastors or full-time Christian workers who say you have hit me right where I have been functioning. I have been basing my relationship with God on the success of my ministry or my performance.

## What Happened to Filthy Rags?
**London/Wiseman:** You just walked into another quote from your book: "I fear that often we Christians begin to think our spiritual growth and success in ministry is due at least in large measure to our own goodness and our hard work. Whatever happened to righteousness as filthy rags?"

**Bridges:** That temptation about goodness and hard work is most real for genuinely committed people, like pastors.

You see, the more committed a person is, the more tempted he is to be pharisaical and to feel self-righteous about his religious activity. Then defective reasoning sets in and he thinks, I'm more committed than these people and I work harder than they do.

It often happens subtly because a deeply committed pastor is kind of pulling his congregation along in many situations.

180

Then it is easy for him to feel self-righteous. I find the more committed Christians become, the more they tend to live by performance and to judge others harshly.

**London/Wiseman:** How can that be?

**Bridges:** Before I make our readers anxious, I am all for discipline and commitment. But many disciplined and committed people are not even born again. An example—the Barcelona Olympic athletes had to be disciplined and committed or they would not have been finalists.

Inasmuch as discipline and commitment are not exclusive Christian virtues, a lot of people who are disciplined by temperament are wholeheartedly committed to different causes. So when those kind of persons accept Christ and learn about holiness and Christian growth, they begin to pursue these character traits with every fiber of their being. Unfortunately, they may depend unconsciously upon the natural discipline in their genes. Then it is easy to judge other people who do not have that natural discipline. These people mistake natural discipline for genuine godliness.

**London/Wiseman:** So, let's propose a scenario from a pastor who enjoys study, loves books, and finds satisfaction in going to his office at 5:30 A.M. where he insists nobody phones him or knocks on his door for the next six hours. Every day he gives himself to that lofty-sounding schedule. Is it possible that there may not be much real devotion to the Lord in that effort but that he is only meeting the needs of his natural discipline?

**Bridges:** That is an excellent example of performance which is likely motivated by natural discipline. As a result, his preaching may be flawless but sterile and academic—prepared but not powerful.

## Transforming Discipline to Devotion
**London/Wiseman:** Say you had a relationship with that pastor and were trying to help him transform discipline to devotion. How could that pastor change? Or should he?

**Bridges:** That is a great choice of words—transform discipline to devotion. First Corinthians 13 is a good place to start; in the first three verses it teaches that we can have knowledge, gifts of speaking and language, faith, zeal, and commitment, but it amounts to precisely nothing—absolute zero—without love.

Then I would suggest to him that his sermons are terrific—well-organized and well-constructed. I would say you do thorough research. But then I would ask him to consider verse 4 where love is patient and kind.

**London/Wiseman:** Then reality sets in.

**Bridges:** Yes. Reality sets in so he does not totally abandon his zealous study habits but begins to work on love—an absolutely essential element of personal holiness. And he questions himself, "How am I going to build love into my ministry?"

**London/Wiseman:** We often ask ourselves how pastors can love people when they have such a busy schedule.

Do you understand that some pastors work sixty, seventy, eighty, ninety hours a week and serve a congregation that is clamoring for attention? Few people realize that an effective pastor creates an increased demand for his time, so he is at it early in the morning and late at night.

The problem: he doesn't have time to fit aloneness with God into this equation. What do you say to him?

**Bridges:** He does not have time not to fit God into his equation. It is as essential as food and water and oxygen for his personal spiritual well-being and for his congregation too. All his success is going to come tumbling down, either in this life or at the judgment, if he does not build personal holiness into his ministry.

When we stand before God to account for what we have done, all ministry without Him is going to be sounding brass and tinkling cymbals. It may have looked good statistically in this life, but how will it really look for eternity?

I am convinced that we cannot build into our people what we do not have in our lives—personal holy character.

## The Real Source for Ministry

**London/Wiseman:** Beautiful. Are you saying there is no way to give the people the spiritual realities of God unless we possess them ourselves?

**Bridges:** Yes—the real "resourcing" for ministry is personal holiness. So I strongly urge overly busy pastors to cut down other ministry activities by an hour every day; then spend that first hour with God where the pastor forgets sermons and people, and prays, "Lord, here I am; what do You have to say to me today?" Effective ministry to people grows out of intimate experiences with God. Consequently, relationship with Him energizes and informs all phases of ministry.

**London/Wiseman:** Our dialogue generates life-giving hope for pastors who have fatigue in their voices, their handwriting, their conversations, and on their faces. This reminder can be revolutionary. In place of performance, they can live in transforming grace.

As we discuss rekindling love for God and the pursuit of personal holiness, we discover a spiritual stamina and supernatural toughness available to pastors, pastors' wives, pastors' families. There is a strength from beyond that flows from through those who are genuinely holy. It provides a significant supernatural strength and insight in the intricacy of their calling and complexities of their pastorates.

All of this means that when a pastor gives first priority to personal holiness, he will be astounded at what he is able to accomplish in his ministry.

**Bridges:** Exactly.

**London/Wiseman:** This enabling power of the Holy Spirit flows through a holy pastor into the agonies and ecstasies of contemporary ministry. That is powerful. Let's try to be specific. How is this to be done?

**Bridges:** About an hour is needed with the Lord each day to feed our souls and to provide energy for ministry.

**London/Wiseman:** You believe it takes an hour a day?

**Bridges:** No question in my mind. I spend 5:45 to 6:45 every morning. Approximately half of that time is spent reading Scripture to allow it to minister to me and to ask the Holy Spirit to speak to me. I read with the question, "Lord, what do You want to say to me this morning?"

**London/Wiseman:** You spend half the time reading the Word and making self-application?

**Bridges:** Yes, and the second half hour is for praying. I pray for the church and the nation. I pray about the assault on the family. Issues that are larger than my own needs.

One of the most important things I do is ask God to keep me on a short leash. I want a tender conscience to keep me from straying in my thought life or to prevent me from rationalizing about little things.

For an example of a short leash — let's say I lead in a church or Christian organization where I have an expense account. Like any businessperson, I face the temptation to fudge on my expenditures when I am away from home. No one intends to be crooked, but it is easy to rationalize that I deserve this.

Maybe you have noticed how extravagant some Christian leaders become when the church or organization is paying the bills — the kind of restaurants they patronize and price of meals they order compared with what they do when it comes out of their own pockets. It is slippery business and easy to dupe ourselves.

Thus, I ask God to give me a tender conscience because, as the Song of Solomon 2:15 says, it is the little foxes that spoil. I believe the battle is won or lost in the little things. If we let little things go, the big things will devour us, maybe even wreck our witness and destroy our relationship with God.

**London/Wiseman:** That is a sound warning.

**Bridges:** I believe God holds those in the ministry to a higher standard. James 3:1 says we will be judged more strictly. I think we must realize we cannot afford to indulge in those little sins.

**London/Wiseman:** Is it fair to say that the pastor who becomes mired down in a fault, a moral indiscretion, sexual infidelity, or tax cheating is likely to be one who has not been pursuing personal holiness?

**Bridges:** Yes. And I do not think it is judging, but merely diagnosing a preventable catastrophe.

**London/Wiseman:** So you think these problems cannot be blamed on childhood, heredity, or environment, but on the simple fact that one did not keep a tight intimate relationship with God?

**Bridges:** That's right, and it does not have to happen.

**London/Wiseman:** How can pastors guard against these destructive downfalls?

**Bridges:** Jesus taught us in the Lord's Prayer to pray to be delivered from temptation. So we should pray every day, "Lord, keep me from temptation. Keep me from the assaults of Satan. And keep me from being blindsided by my own unworthy desires."

Jesus also advised us to watch and pray that we do not enter into temptation. I believe this watching is our own vigilant scrutiny of our lives, which includes being brutally scrupulous with ourselves. The praying part expresses dependence upon God. Both reliance on God and a prudent watch on ourselves are demanded.

**London/Wiseman:** So you consider a pastor's personal holiness to be his first responsibility both to his church and to himself, no matter how many hours he works or what pressures he experiences?

**Bridges:** Yes. It is his first obligation and also his extraordinary source of spiritual vitality.

## Negotiate Priorities with Church Leaders

**Bridges:** Let me add a word to pastors who may be frustrated by what I have said. Share your concern for time for pursuing personal holiness with your governing group—those leaders who could ultimately say you have thirty days to get out of town.

Help them see that your walk with God is your greatest duty to your own soul and your most pressing obligation to the church. Help them understand you have a limited number of hours and that you have to give first priority to this connection with God. Ask them to help you set priorities in your ministry. Seek their evaluation with the question, "What is most important for the church?" And then share what you think is most essential.

**RISK FACTORS**

Of nearly 1,500 responses, we have found that over half of the pastors surveyed do not meet regularly with a prayer partner. Sadly, 1 out of 4 do not have a trusted friend in ministry. And surprisingly, only 20% have at least 2 paid ministerial staff members.

Focus on the Family Survey

Negotiate priorities with them. You may think sermon preparation is tops, and they may consider discipling six men as lay leaders to be first. In this evolutionary effort, you will soon run out of time with an unfinished list of things that still needs doing. But it is important and enlightening for everyone on the leadership team to have a part in the decision. As a result, some tasks may not get done or else someone else in the church will have to do them.

Pastors often mistakenly underestimate the laypersons' understanding of spiritual realities. Any spiritually alert lay leader wants his pastor to be a developing disciple of Jesus who is growing in Christlikeness. Trust them with the fact you want to pursue personal holiness. In most instances they will be supportive or even generous with helping you find ways to do it. And the discussion creates a commitment to follow through on your part.

**London/Wiseman:** That suggestion furnishes a doable way to take responsibility for your personal holiness and at the same time to share the ministry of the church. Now, let us apply this idea of pursuing personal holiness in practical, nontheoretical ways.

Here is a recurring apprehension from a pastor's letter: "I'm preacher, counselor, secretary, and sometimes maintenance man at our small church. I carry a heavy burden for the spiritual and emotional well-being of my flock. Satan is always attacking in one way or another. Sometimes I do not have energy to fight the battle anymore." How can he find help?

**Bridges:** I think he needs a vacation with God where he repairs his relationship with the Lord—a time to recharge his spiritual and emotional batteries. A family tour of Disneyland won't cure this fatigue in his soul.

**London/Wiseman:** That expression—repair his relationship with the Lord—says it just right.

**Bridges:** This pastor needs to view his problem like a serious physical illness where he backs off from some commitments for a period of time or maybe forever. If he had serious surgery, he would be out of work for six weeks. That is just the way it is when the doctor says, "No, you cannot go back to work." Why should it be different for a fatigued pastor?

Without proper care his spiritual exhaustion will only get worse. And his weariness is not going to be repaired by one hour per day; the hour a day is maintenance for the spiritually healthy pastor. This man needs intensive care for his soul.

**London/Wiseman:** You think this pastor could get well by continuing his regular routine at a slower pace?

**Bridges:** No way—he is on an endless treadmill. He will probably get much worse without resolute intervention. His condition can become chronic or spiritually life-threatening. Either way, he is in trouble and needs prompt assistance.

**London/Wiseman:** Another letter from a devoted pastor: "My greatest worry is to set a consistent Christlike example—first before my wife and children, and then before the congregation. I truly long to be a spiritual leader, to be someone who, by virtue of his intimate relationship with Christ, greatly influences others to be like Him."

That sounds like a laudable goal, but is he taking too much obligation on himself?

**Bridges:** I think his goal is worthy and achievable. But I suggest to every pastor that they be honest about their own weaknesses and failures. I have been a Christian for forty-four years, and the pastors who ministered most effectively to me sometimes came to the pulpit and said, "Hey, folks, I don't have anything to say today."

**London/Wiseman:** Those are the nightmare times for pastors.

**Bridges:** The goal of the pastor-parishioner pilgrimage is to pursue holiness together. I remember one Sunday our pastor said, "I was ready to come to church this morning and my wife wasn't ready. I got upset with her because she was going to make me late getting to church." By telling us that from the pulpit he helped us see that he was one of us and that we must pursue holiness together. Now he was a godly man, and he didn't tell us every time something went wrong in his life, but by being open on occasions, he came across as a person who is eager to be like Christ. He conveyed both spiritual eagerness and day-by-day realities.

**London/Wiseman:** So you think being transparent is useful for a pastor?

**Bridges:** Transparent—that's the idea exactly.

**London/Wiseman:** It is really preaching confessionally when a pastor is willing to stand before his people and say, "My feet of clay sure showed this week."

**Bridges:** Transparent and confessional—those are liberating acts for the pastor and for believers under his care.

**London/Wiseman:** Let's consider one more letter: "My greatest challenge is not to become so involved in administration, visitation, and other phases of the work of the Lord that I do not have quality time for getting to know the Lord of the work."

It is easy to forget that it is the Lord's work, and we let it become our work. How can pastors keep themselves reminded that it is the Lord's work they are doing?

**Bridges:** I use visual reminders. I have a pen with a pedestal on my desk, so I write a Scripture reference on a small slip of paper, like John 15:5: "Apart from Me you can do nothing." Then I tape that Bible reference across the pedestal of that pen so I see John 15:5 every time I look at the pen.

Another especially useful Scripture is the well-known story in Luke 10 where Martha was distracted over her business while Mary was sitting at the feet of Jesus. On that occasion, Jesus said to Martha, "One thing is needed" (v. 7). *One thing!*

As an overworked pastor, I might tape that phrase—ONE THING—or the reference to the dashboard of my car or on the pedestal of my desk pen.

Another passage is Psalm 27:4: "One thing I ask of the Lord, that I may dwell in the house of the Lord all the days of my life, to gaze upon the beauty of the Lord and to seek Him in His temple." Psalm 27:4 is my number one prayer request for myself.

**London/Wiseman:** If you could only say one thing to the average pastor, what would it be? What advice do you have to help a pastor become a better pastor, husband, father, and Christian?

**Bridges:** I would go to Enoch, who is mentioned only a few times in the Bible (e.g., Gen. 5; Heb. 11; and Jude 14). Enoch walked with God in Genesis 5, and he pleased God in Hebrews 11.

Enoch is my favorite Bible character because he clearly

stands for those two things—walking with God and pleasing God. Every pastor can do both—no one can stop him. And every pastor needs the resources that come through such an intimate relationship with God.

**London/Wiseman:** What a strength for ministry! Though we do not know if Enoch built any prominent churches or influenced any great movements, he walked with God and was pleasing to Him. Every pastor can walk with God and be pleasing to Him.

## Helps for Pursuing Personal Holiness

Jerry Bridges' energizing message must be heard by all pastors. For too long, pastors have shortchanged themselves by separating personal holiness from the practice of ministry, competency from character, and service from spirituality. To think of ways to bring the inner and outer worlds together, meet Michael Messner.

Michael Messner was a typical minister in the making who earned good grades, married well on the day after college graduation, and was voted by classmates as the "most likely to succeed." And when church leaders came to recruit pastors during his last semester in seminary, he had his choice of several strong entry-level churches.

Michael and his wife, Suzanne, moved to their first church and did well for two years. But he soon missed the academic stimulus of the seminary and felt trapped by the repetition of ministry. He hit an invisible wall like a high-spirited jogger and didn't know how to get around it.

Changing environments seemed to be his only answer. With his charisma and outstanding academic achievements, it was easy to move to another church in another state. But unfortunately he had to take himself with him, so the same pattern developed again: great start, boredom, frustration, loneliness, and an eagerness new challenges and scenery. Soon the "fast-tracker" fizzled again, moved on to become a counselor in a mental health clinic and grieves over what happened to his dreams for parish ministry.

Recently Michael and Suzanne met a lovely retired couple, Tom and Sarah Kratz, who shared satisfying pastoral ministry for forty years in three churches. As the two couples developed a strong friendship in spite of the age differences, Sarah asked Suzanne, "What did Michael do in his ministry to feed his soul?" She continued, "Tom and I found joy for the journey because we discovered early on that he had to keep his soul fat, or he had nothing to give people that mattered much. So he committed time and effort to developing a holy character, and I encouraged him to do so because he was more fun to live with when he was spiritually strong and fulfilled."

Sarah is right. Ultimately, there is nothing more powerful or influential in the church than a fulfilled pastor who does his work with an inner zest, rooted in a pursuit of personal holiness with God. The following suggestions help to answer the question *how*.

- *Recognize Your Need for Power to Control*
Maybe Dostoyevsky is right, "Without God we are too strong for each other." Organizational control can be enticing and destructive, even to spiritually minded people. But abuse of administrative, ecclestical, or spiritual authority frequently conditions fair-minded followers to passivity at the same time it is withering the power grabber's soul. People do not stop following a leader because he is spiritually strong or persevering. Rather they quit or quietly turn to apathy and mediocrity because they believe the leader is controlling or ego-driven.

Though the Bible expects a pastor to be an overseer, it never permits manipulation, conniving, or dictatorship. In the work of God, leadership privilege or position should be held loosely while the work is taken seriously. The Bible trusts the pastor with authority for achievement but this authority was never intended for ego gratification or selfish pyramiding of supremacy.

Power seduces pastors in every sized situation. A little organizational authority turns some mild-mannered ministers into controlling tyrants. Positional power hopelessly locks others into trivia where they do everything because their egos want to be in charge. Either way, the controller suffers spiritual heart damage, and the congregation's creativity is stifled.

Four lies about power sabotage a pastor's efforts to be like Christ: (1) I'm special and not subject to entanglements others face; (2) I don't play by the rules—not even God's; (3) I deserve my position in the will of God; and (4) I'm brighter and holier than those I lead.

Far better to ask for help and share success. That's the pattern of Jesus which gets more work done and, in the process, frees the pastor's time and emotions to develop his inner world. The bailout from this in-charge enslavement is to be sure both the assignment as well as ourselves are continually given to the trusted control of God.

● *Use Devotion As a Catalyst for Discipline*
Although duty, obligation, and accountability are part of ministry, it is deep-seated devotion to Christ which gives discipline meaning. It is a foundational principle of effective ministry that devotion fuels discipline fully as much as love sends us out to earn a living for our families. Love energizes discipline—that's the secret that makes Christian obligations satisfying. Pleasing the Father is always easier when it is inspired by devotion, rather than required by responsibility. For example, quiet times are required for a meaningful ministry, but they have much more meaning when they are warm, caring conversations with a trusted Friend. And Bible reading is always more rewarding when it is viewed as reading a love letter from God.

● *Resist the "Too Busy" Syndrome*
Obligations and expectations keep a pastor's calendar loaded. Inasmuch as a pastor cannot escape a datebook, why not use it for what really matters? Why not schedule time with God just as intentionally as you schedule the Sunday morning worship service? Bridges' idea that the busy pastor is the one

who most needs time alone with God is an ideal every pastor must make operational.

● *Refurbish Your Original Vision*
As the years roll on, the magnet of meaning which first attracts the pastor to ministry can be forgotten. Then without continuous miraculous enablement, the pastor's work turns into trifling "do-goodism." On the contrary, a supernatural vision for the work enlivens ministry and makes it fruitful. This "something beyond" renews vision and causes ministry to impact people in life-changing ways like nothing else can. And it also makes the pastor's work seem worthwhile even on dark days. Like Enoch, cultivating God's friendship gives importance to everything else.

To refocus the vision, keep close to the basics of faith. Return often to the vision given you when you started your present assignment. Polish the original vision. Preach it. Write about it. Be controlled by it. Celebrate the satisfaction ministry brings into your life. Relish ministry as a marvelous way of life and make it true. Remember what God promised when He called you.

● *Drop All Pretense*
Because pastors are public figures, they live much of their lives on platforms and before the watchful eye of crowds. Thus, it becomes easy to believe their own press releases or the genteel compliments people sometimes shower upon them. As a result, an entire ministry can become a lie. It creates an impression of lofty service to God and people, when it is actually the pastor's ego seeking its own satisfaction.

In such situations, pastors live in fantasy, sham, and hype—all make-believe illusions. They delude themselves by overestimating their worth to the church, commitment to individual prayer, and faithfulness in applying the Bible to their own lives. All rubbish. Such self-deception produces spiritual rigor mortis and destroys the spiritual vigor of a congregation.

Face the facts: pretending to be holy takes more effort than the real thing; pretending to be generous costs almost as much as the genuine article; and pretending to be loving is harder than being loving. It takes more effort to look back over one's shoulder to be sure of a good impression than it does to do the right thing for the right reason which always produces a positive impression.

Jesus honors honesty, but hates pretense. He even challenges us to make our speech, attitudes, and actions match.

● *Seek Clarifying Solitude*
Solitude may be hard to find and harder still to face because we may not like what we discover about ourselves at the quiet place. Withdrawal from our public life tends to bring buried issues and toxic relations into candid focus.

An hour of solitude where "we take captive every thought to make it obedient to Christ" (2 Cor. 10:5) clears spiritual, emotional, and relational cobwebs out of the corners of our lives. In some quiet corner of life, every pastor needs what the Quakers call "centering down on Christ." Seasons of solitude with God enable us to see life and ministry accurately.

● *Review Patterns of Ministry*
In ministry, direction determines outcomes and patterns govern productivity. Thus, a pastor must intentionally invest energy and effort in what he wants the years of his ministry to do for God. He must commit to the impact he wants to make on believers under his spiritual care. He must know what he wants his work to reveal.

To review and refocus the direction of ministry, ask yourself these questions. Where do you want your ministry to go? Is your preaching happy or judgmental? Does your counseling help people to Christlike wholeness, or is it rigidly restrictive? Is your leadership liberating or enslaving? Do people come to redeeming friendship with the Heavenly Father because of your ministry, or are their fears about God reinforced? What is the direction of your ministry, and is it going where you want it to go? Intentional faithfulness to your vision for ministry is the key.

● *Take God into Your Realities*

There is overwhelming evidence that ministry is tougher now than ever before. That is the explicit reason why it has to be done well. Since your ministry is linked to Omnipotence, look beyond the problems to the Power, beyond the scarcity to the Abundance, and beyond the hurt to the Healer.

As every pastor knows, those who try to do ministry in their own strength are swamped by minutia or stressed to the breaking point. The load, however, lightens significantly when all the resources of God are focused like a laser beam on our best efforts. Amazing achievement results.

Taking God into the realities of ministry also helps identify our distortions which can so easily wreck ministry. Such a God-closeness enables the pastor to see if he is putting the complex pieces of of the ministry together accurately. Who among us has not come to a false conclusion that slowed or squelched ministry? Perhaps pastors need to consider an additional beatitude: Blessed are those who allow God to help them see things as they are.

This process is not meant to deny difficulties, play down problems, or use empty words to pacify crises. Rather, it is meant to take the Lord of the universe into everyday ministry—to bring Him into the midst of our misunderstandings, overly tight budgets, feelings of despair, and sense of isolation. It makes real the promises, "I am with you always" (Matt. 28:20) and "Never will I leave you; never will I forsake you" (Heb. 13:5). It often starts with a powerful five-second prayer break in difficult situations: "God, please see me through this difficulty to victory." And indeed He does.

## THE CONTEMPORARY CHALLENGE
## FOLLOW THE FATHER'S AGENDA

Pursue personal holiness at any cost as a favor to yourself *and* your ministry. Such an intimate connection with Christ revitalizes your motivation for service and provides the raw materials of tenacity and fulfillment in ministry. It is the cornerstone of productivity and the underpinning for satisfaction in ministry. Personal holiness keeps a pastor's soul in shape.

Compelling demands of present-day ministry depletes a pastor's spiritual stamina, so he feels dry, empty, and exhausted. But there is a life-saving alternative. It is an intimacy with Christ which invigorates a pastor so he can victoriously meet the rigors of his task with restored focus and vigor.

Though most pastors know something about personal holiness in a theoretical, idealistic way, they may not know how to effectively initiate intimacy with Christ. Think of the hindrances in your own history, environment, eccentricities, fatigue, and fears that keep you from reaching beyond what you have experienced.

But the first step to discover growth in personal holiness is to move from vagueness to specifics. For physically overworked and spiritually undernourished pastors, intimacy with Christ can start to flow from many faith formation tributaries. Henri Nouwen, the Catholic encourager of Christian leaders, offers a starting list of three: "contemplative reading of the word of God, a silent listening to the voice of God, and trusting obedience to a spiritual guide."[3] What a faith building list!

With crystal clear discernment concerning personal holiness for pastors, Nouwen suggests, "Instead of taking the words of Scripture apart, we should bring them together in our innermost being; instead of wondering if we agree or disagree, we should wonder which words are directly spoken to us and connect directly with our most personal story."[4] A similar personal application and accountability can be applied to listening to God and trusting obedience to a spiritual guide. Nouwen's coaching simply suggests that pastors lay down analysis and diagnosis to take health restoring prescriptions.

In the midst of the frightening hazards pastors face in our time, the pursuit of personal holiness is God's wake-up call to move us from professional religion to personal faith. Such a pursuit will revitalize our sense of direction, stimulate our confidence in society's need for righteousness, and intensify our passion for doing God's work in this kind of world.

Unleashed in our inner world, who knows where personal holiness might take us in our outer world.

The world and the church await to follow spiritual leaders who demonstrate and enjoy personal intimacy with Christ in the minute particulars of their lives and ministry. A reactivated faith that laughs at risks and overpowers the hazards modern ministers face might start with renewed intimacy with Christ.

## RENEWAL STRATEGIES
## DEEPENING YOUR INTIMACY WITH CHRIST

✔ Recognize Your Need for Power to Control
✔ Use Devotion As a Catalyst for Discipline
✔ Resist the "Too Busy" Syndrome
✔ Refurbish Your Original Vision
✔ Drop All Pretense
✔ Seek Clarifying Solitude
✔ Review Patterns of Ministry
✔ Take God into Your Realities

TEN

# Let Laypeople Help*

"Let the pastor's family out of the fishbowl. They're human too." — a bishop from Florida

I
n churches large and small, the pastoral family is always a delightful topic of conversation: what they wear, what they drive, where they go on vacation, how the kids behave, and what their house looks like. Though many church folks may not stop to view this from the other side, ministers call it "life in the fishbowl."

Pastors have reason to feel that congregations not only hold a set of high expectations, but intend to help the pastor and family live up to it. Now, that's pressure! In more than a few churches, of course, the pastoral household never measures up. The inability to be "perfect goldfish" causes pastors to

---

*This chapter is adapted from *Pastors at Risk* by H.B. London, Jr. with Dean Merrill, a booklet which is available from Focus on the Family for distribution to key lay leaders.

In this chapter we acknowledge and celebrate the important link between lay leaders and pastors in contemporary churches. For lay leaders, it suggests strategies you can use to strengthen your pastor in these risky times. Pastors, at the same time, are urged to challenge laypersons to assume more significant ministry roles through the church. Let's multiply our combined effectiveness for Christ by implementing these ideas into the ministry of your church.

leave a church prematurely or even leave the ministry altogether.

What can church members do to prevent this? The first step is to realize that a pastor is not a goldfish. Have you ever taken time to watch those beautiful creatures swimming gracefully in their confines? They seem so serene, safe, and well-fed as they cruise from one side of the bowl to the other. But do they enjoy being on display twenty-four hours a day? What do they think about the piercing eyes of the outside world that stare at them?

## Here's How It Was in H.B.'s Family

"I was a preacher's kid in a family filled with preachers, and I've been a pastor myself for thirty-one years. My parents never lived next door to the church we served, but I had grandparents and uncles and aunts who did. Even as a young boy, I could not understand why church people did not respect my relatives' privacy. It was almost as though the pastor was just the caretaker of the parsonage, and when folks needed to use the phone, get a drink of water, use the restroom — or just pop in for a chat — they did. In fact, I scarcely remember my grandfather without a tie and suit coat. He knew what the church expected of him, and so, from early morning until late in the evening he wore a coat and tie.

"The churches my wife, Beverley, and I served were wonderful to us and our two boys. They afforded us special opportunities and marvelous kindness — but I did notice that smaller congregations seemed to scrutinize their pastors more than larger ones. I began in a church with fewer than 100 members and concluded my pastoral ministry in a church of more than 3,000. In my first pastorate I remember having to get the board's permission not only to paint the parsonage, but even what color to use. Needless to say, as soon as we (with the help of my mom and dad) could scrape up the funds for a down payment on our own home, we did. Unfortunately, that was not until our fourth year in the ministry."

## Here's How It Was in Neil's Pastoral Pilgrimage

"My faith journey, rooted in a small church and a lay home, began when I was born the first child of young parents committed to cultivating homegrown faith. Through good times and lean years, for more than fifty years, our family was an integral part of a small Detroit Eastside congregation that started as a house church in our neighborhood.

"During economic depression days, the Dubay Street Church's survival required intense involvement and sacrificial giving from everyone—the strenuous task of keeping the church doors open kept us in top-notch spiritual shape. I was led to Christ and called to preach there.

"In that church, everyone was part of a big spiritual family where we probably made unreasonable demands on our pastors, though we did not know it. Struggles, victories, rituals, births, weddings, and funerals bonded us so there were no secrets—everybody knew everybody else's business and talked about it. I honestly can't remember hearing expectations discussed.

"Since then, thirty-seven years of close associations with pastors make me see life through a pastor's eyes. Twenty of those years have been invested in pastoral service to various sized congregations in California, Washington, Colorado, and Florida. My journey in ministry, in addition to being unofficial ombudsman for pastors at denominational headquarters and two colleges, has included assignments as college professor, academic administrator, and pastoral development director for 5,000 pastors. In these relationships, I have experienced an invigorating interplay between helping pastors develop and being shaped by them at the same time. All these connections with pastors convince me that thousands want to break through real and imagined barriers into remarkable achievement.

"But to do it, they need the affection and affirmation of laypersons. They need admiration, generosity, and friendship. They need lay partners in ministry to look after their well-being."

The care and emotional feeding of the pastor and family need not be complex, just intentional and regular. Following are suggestions that any layperson can spearhead. These ideas can make an important difference in the lives of pastors and their long-term ability to minister to you and your church.

## Salary and Retirement Benefits
The Bible says, "The worker deserves his wages" (Luke 10:7). A pastor should be compensated on par with the people being served and with other ministers in the same community. The old philosophy of a pastor "suffering for Jesus' sake" does not hold water, especially if the people are able to provide for the pastoral needs.

Salaries do vary from one section of the country to another, but many pastors are living below the poverty level. They usually aren't complaining, but they're barely existing. Leadership in every church should be more concerned about the physical and fiscal well-being of the pastor and family than about any other area, with the exception of the pastor's level of spirituality. If merit raises cannot be given every year, at least a cost-of-living increase should be granted.

One of the saddest commentaries on the church is the way some pastors are treated upon retirement. The horror stories that come from many of our retired ministers are dreadful. If your pastor does not understand the importance of retirement benefits, please provide some reputable counsel. It is not the pastor's responsibility alone to plan for the future—the congregation has a role to play as well.

In all these areas, the point is not to make anyone rich. It is to give a pastor the freedom to minister instead of worry.

## Time for Restoration and Relaxation
In a pastor's life, the "light" is always on. There's always another phone call to make, parishioner to visit, sermon to prepare, funeral to conduct, or wedding to perform—not to mention a family to manage. The list is endless.

All pastors need time away with their families as well as

time alone with their God. One very popular minister in the United States compares many pastors to "wagons with their wheels coming off, heading for the ditch." If your pastor is to do better than this, free time is a must. Specifically this means:

*A day off!* Let pastors pick the best day for them, and then respect their privacy. Don't call. Don't stop by. Don't interrupt—unless, of course, there is a true emergency.

One frustrated pastor writes: "The issue I believe that church people—pastors and laypeople—need to hear from you is boundaries. The pastor and the people need to realize that the pastor does not solve their problems. We are not God, and we are not omnicompetent."

*Vacation.* Pastors should have at least two weeks each year, and because they are asked to serve on so many holidays, they should also receive replacement days for those occasions. The lay leaders should not only insist on the pastor and family taking the vacation, but should assist in finding and funding pulpit supply when necessary.

One of the saddest stories we ever heard was about the church board that docked the pastor for vacation time while he attended the funeral of his daughter, who had been killed in an automobile accident. A church like that does not even deserve a pastor. All pastors should have personal and bereavement days.

Vacation time should be determined by the number of years the pastor has served in full-time ministry—not the tenure at a particular church. For instance, someone who has been a pastor for fifteen years should receive at least four weeks' vacation, despite the fact that he or she may have been in the present post only two years.

*Conferences and retreats.* So often pastors go dry from giving and giving without any spiritual nurturing of their own. Who pastors the pastor?

When possible, the church should provide at least one opportunity a year for its pastor to be fed. This might be a conference, a spiritual retreat, or a denominational function.

Every church will be better served if its leader is filled with new insights and motivation.

*Dates.* Spending time alone with a spouse is essential to a healthy union. Married pastors need it too. It is exciting to hear that more pastors and their spouses are dating again — at least once each month.

Caring parishioners can offer themselves for babysitting duty. It is a proven fact that when a pastor and spouse are communicating and happy in their relationship, their effectiveness in the church is greatly enhanced.

## Prayer, Love, and Encouragement

*Pray for your pastor!* This is, in fact, the very best thing you can do (1 Tim. 2:1-2). Not only is prayer the greatest show of support, but it is also a catalyst for unity. It is difficult to pray for someone and be critical of them at the same time. A great degree of discord in the church today results from inadequate prayer. People have allowed differences to divide them.

Prayer not only changes things, but it empowers pastors to be the persons God called them to be. Of all the phrases that thrill a pastor, the greatest is when someone in the congregation says, "Pastor, I'm praying for you."

*Love and encourage your pastor.* Don't let little things get blown out of proportion. Sometimes this happens to the point of dividing a church and even triggering the pastor's dismissal. This results in a kind of pain for everyone that never goes away.

As a church body, we need to show the world and one another that good conquers evil and that love is the greatest force in the world. Jesus said it is easy to say I love you, but love needs to be exhibited. How? Show it! Send a note of encouragement. Remember your pastor's birthday and anniversary. Recognize your pastor's employment anniversary each year in some tangible way (1 Thes. 5:11). Launch a Pastor Appreciation Sunday each year. Perhaps you might even provide each lay leader with a copy of this book so your vision can be shared.

It can almost be guaranteed that, in return, your pastor will give the very best to you and the congregation. Encouragement begets faithful service.

In many ways, the laity makes or breaks a pastor. You have an awesome responsibility to see that your pastor can stand before you with heart and soul prepared to preach the Word of God. To do that, your pastor's mind should be free of distraction, controversy, and worry about money.

**Be Willing to Dream**

Many letters from pastors describe their dreams for their congregations. You can almost hear a cry for people committed to fulfilling the Great Commission. Many pastors are literally at their wits' end because so many people are simply not involved in the major assignment of the body of Christ—spiritual reproduction. "Tell me how," pastors plead, "to get my people to realize that spiritual reproduction is not an option; it is expected of every person who calls himself by the name of Christ."

The great mission we are facing cannot be clergy-driven. The clergy must teach and lead, but the laity must respond out of love for God and people. The battle against abortion, pornography, and immorality, and the struggle for "family values" must be fought by convinced believers—not simply committed clergy. For this to happen, there must be a renewal within the church. The church must repent and feel sorrow for its unwillingness to be "salt and light" (Matt. 5:13-16).

The most exhilarating moments for a pastor do not come from large crowds, great sermons, or successful finance campaigns, but rather from a layperson who has been touched by the power of God and says, "Pastor, I really want to make a difference in my world. Will you help me? Will you train me? Will you pray for me?"

Wow! If you want to take your pastor to a new plateau in effectiveness, offer yourself in this way. Be open to new ideas. More than ever before, your pastor has access to resources and new concepts from the world's greatest religious leaders. So when he proposes ideas and dreams for your congregation that might seem a bit innovative or grandiose, keep an open mind. Work to keep your pastor dreaming and alive. Don't allow his creative juices to dry up.

Phrases like "that won't work," "it costs too much," and "we've always done it that way" are deadly. The Holy Spirit is the author of dreams. If your pastor is in touch with God's Spirit, allow the opportunity to witness His touch on the life of your church. Don't be guilty of squelching the Spirit simply because the dreams and hopes may seem farfetched or unreachable.

How sad it is when the power structure within the congregation will not allow the Spirit to bring renewal. It's hard for human control to entertain the thought that God may want to be "doing a new thing" where you worship (Isa. 43:18-19). But let your pastor lead. Let your minister be the shepherd as God ordained.

## Realistic Expectations
The above is not meant to portray a one-way street. Giving is an important word for your pastor as well as for you. If you are taking the above steps, here is what you have a right to expect from your pastor.

● He should provide a full-time effort, if he is not employed outside the church. It seems unlikely that any pastor could do justice to the position in less than fifty hours a week. For some, it might take longer; for some, it might take less. But to cover the long list of a minister's duties takes time, and lots of it (1 Thes. 2:10-12).

● Your pastor may not be the best preacher in the world,

but he should never step before an audience unprepared. That takes reading, Bible study, prayer, and practice (2 Tim. 4:2).

● A shepherd should know the sheep and their needs. In other words, the pastor should care for you, be a good listener, express compassion, and seek after wisdom (John 10:14).

● Your pastor need not "know it all," but he must be secure enough to search for answers, even if the answers lie with another pastor (Prov. 4:10-12).

● Your pastor needs to be a person of faith and prayer. A prayerless pastor is a powerless pastor (Matt. 17:20-21).

● Your pastor should be a person of courage, willing to confront evil and injustice. A cowardly pastor is not in close fellowship with the Lord. Pastoring is not for the faint of heart (2 Tim. 1:7; Josh. 1:9).

● Your pastor and family should be an example to the congregation. No, they do not need to be perfect! The kids need not be the best behaved in the church. The spouse need not head every committee. But they do need to be a family committed to Scripture's principles regarding family life (Eph. 5:21–6:4; 1 Tim. 3:1-7; Titus 1:6-9).

● Your pastor should spend time training and equipping others to assist in the ministry of pastoral care. We are not all called to be evangelists, but we all are expected to know how to share our faith. Your pastor must prepare you for the responsibilities of lay ministry by helping you find your gifts (2 Tim. 2:2).

● Your pastor should teach the value of Christian stewardship. If you grasp the significance of tithing your time, talent, and treasure, it will not only open up God's special resources for you and your family, but it will also ensure the blessing of God upon your congregation. He promised to pour His blessings upon you (Mal. 3:10; 2 Cor. 9:6-8) in response to your stewardship.

● Your pastor must be a person of integrity. There should be no hint of immorality (Eph. 5:3-5).

● You should expect your pastor to be vulnerable and transparent, willing to admit when mistakes have been made, and committed to continued growth in every aspect (Ps. 139:23-24).

• Most important of all, your pastor must be committed to personal holiness. Too many clergy are successful by the world's standards but woefully lacking when it comes to a relationship with God (Ps. 51:10-12; Rom. 3:22).

## THE CONTEMPORARY CHALLENGE
## STRENGTH FOR THE SWIM

Life in the fishbowl for your pastor and family is reality. It is not an easy assignment. Satan's task is to hinder and undermine those who have been called by God to represent Him as shepherds of the sheep. Pastors can survive life in the fishbowl, but not without your tender love, prayer, and encouragement.

When we look into the pastoral aquarium these days, we see more and more of our colleagues floating slowly to the top—just like goldfish that have died. Many of our colleagues tell us they are burned out, worn out, frustrated, and fatigued.

If ever there was a time when pastors needed to know they are viewed with encouragement and affirmation, it is now. As Aaron and Hur held up the arms of Moses when he grew weary, every pastor needs the stabilizing forces of family and the laypeople in the church family to stand alongside in understanding and camaraderie.

# ELEVEN

# Twelve Steps to Overcoming the Risks

*Is there a way a young guy like me can make ministry count today; even with all the problems?—a novice pastor from Georgia*

S
piritual dryness and emotional starvation are occupational land mines for pastors who do their work continually in a world of half-hearted commitments, moral bankruptcies, devastating sins, and dysfunctional people.

Their situation can easily become hypnotic, so that they see only problems with no hope in sight. Then blaming others or suffering in stoic silence wastes emotional energy that could be used more constructively. These foes—dryness and starvation—are hard to recognize, and it is difficult to imagine what havoc they will trigger tomorrow, next week, and into the new century.

Some strong corrective action is needed immediately. But diagnosing accomplishes nothing without a remedy. What, then, can be done? Who can do it? Who should do it? And what is the prognosis after medication, surgery, or rehabilitation is started?

Consider several possible sources for solutions. Help will not come from church structures—they frequently cause monstrous complications for pastors without intending to do so. Theological educators cannot do it because nothing in their experience or training provides a frame of reference for teaching students how to deal with times like these. Culture and society, grossly misinformed about ministry, assume most pastors are counterfeits and charlatans. And laypersons in the churches are simply not fully aware of the risks pastors experience. Thus, assistance cannot be expected to come from any of these infrastructures.

Where, then, can pastors find help? Perhaps the best hope is ministers themselves. Apparently, they are the only change agents who are aware enough to correct the problem. And no other group is likely to feel the problem so keenly or have more interest in finding a solution.

The positive resources they already possess, if properly used, could alleviate the present predicament quickly: a Bible in their hands, God's love in their hearts, a passionate will to do right in their souls, and an energized commitment to win their world in their plans.

Examine the other choices: Curse the darkness and live in passive acquiescence. Accept festering inner rage for the predicament. Carry protest placards. Raise a new generation in pastors' homes who resents what their fathers' calling does to their lives.

None of these possibilities sound useful, or attractive. Therefore, does it not follow that improvements must be initiated by pastors themselves? Such an effort could be difficult because this self-directed process could be awkward, discomforting, and self-serving in appearance. In reality, however, a frontline attack will shape the whole future of ministry and contour what the church becomes in the new century.

Does it not make sense for pastors to band together to overpower the risks? And if the answer is yes, what kind of a person, leader, and Christian will the pastor for this new day have to be? What attributes and actions will encourage this necessary and satisfying bond between personal piety and professional competence?

## Step 1: Resist Personal Spiritual Power Leakage

Like the necessity of oxygen for human life or gasoline for an
automobile, a pastor's intimacy with Christ is the irreducible
minimum for useful ministry. Without personal faith shining
through all expressions of his ministry, a pastor is an empty
echo of what God intends him to be. Everything in ministry
depends on the pastor's personal faith.

No spiritual leader can be productive who is not holy. Jesus
Himself is the inner vitality for ministry. Mark it down; our
Lord was absolutely correct when He warned we could do
nothing without Him.

Admittedly, it is easy to almost unknowingly blur the differences between personal faith and professional performance.
Merely standing close to spiritual fires every minute of every
day does not make one a vibrant believer. Without clear personal faith, a pastor soon becomes shallow, his vision superficial, his influence minimal, and his satisfaction near zero. He
becomes a pathetic imitation of the real thing.

But perpetual demands militate against personal piety. Obligations for so many public prayers make it easy for the pastor to bypass wholehearted engagement in his private praying. No ministry is more powerless than that of a pastor who
seldom prays personally.

The care of souls can be rendered in the pastor's office with
trifling compassion and little Scripture or prayer. Such an
empty effort is often a poor simulation of secular counseling
and a shoddy excuse for pastoral care. It is the pastor's personal relationship with Jesus that makes his counseling
uniquely different from the work of all other helping professionals.

Hospital calling by the pastor can be done in a routine way
without getting too involved in the patient's pain. A pleasant
bedside manner with a professional flair and a ready smile
produces a pleasing public image. But without the pastor's
personal faith, the hospital visit is merely social with no physical or spiritual healing.

The preaching ministry must also be considered. If Sunday's sermon is worth hearing, it must be a distinctive connection of biblical research, systematized doctrine, skilled speaking, and accurate exegesis of the world where people live. Blending these factors is a big enough order without adding personal piety, but the addition is absolutely indispensable. Like a lawyer in the courtroom or a surgeon in the operating room, the pastor in his pulpit must have his skills honed for maximum effectiveness. But no matter how skilled or experienced the pastor may be, his effort will be only empty rhetoric if the personal faith dimension is missing.

To be genuinely productive, all of ministry must integrate personal piety and painstaking competence. The techniques for feeding one's soul are not so important as the sources. Eugene H. Peterson makes a strong argument that ministry cannot be shaped by God without three connecting angles — Scripture, prayer, and accountability to a soul friend.[1]

Such an alive intimacy with God makes us different from all other professionals. It prompts people to listen actively to our preaching. And it inspires them to call on us in their crises. Nothing the pastor does has lasting value unless it is nourished by his own closeness to God.

No one can force a pastor to feed his own faith, and no one can keep him from it. The temptation of professional performance is one of the most deadly perils a pastor faces. But when these inner resources energize the soul, pastoring is one of the most gratifying works in the world. The fantastic serendipities are fulfillment, exhilaration, and zeal for ministry.

## Step 2: Commit to Contentment and Change

Contentment and change — how can these words be "shoehorned" into the same sentence? By their essence, contentment seems to encourage a "do-not-rock-the-boat" mentality, and change seems to signal discontentment. But the two ideas can be on friendly terms in the pastorate.

Contentment — gratitude for what we have — keeps us from chafing about what we do not have. A lay leader helps us see

211

this idea from a refreshing perspective, "We are embarrassed by what little we are able to do for our pastor, but when he expresses thanks for what we do, it makes most of us try harder to improve his lot in life." Discontentment, conversely, slows change to a snail's pace or stops it dead.

Discontentment for some people is a perpetual habit in marriage, family, or ministry; it is a costly attitude that robs them of the joy of living. The Apostle Paul shares the secret of a satisfying life: "I have learned to be content whatever the circumstances. I know what it is to be in need, and I know what it is to have plenty. I have learned the secret of being content in any and every situation, whether well fed or hungry, whether living in plenty or in want" (Phil. 4:11-12). Existing opportunities and privileges are hard to see when we are stressed by a truckload of limitations and hindrances.

Contentment and change are also tied together in another way, so when a leader shows contentment with what he has, he gains credibility for asking people to do better. Subsequently, the contented pastor usually asks for and gets change that benefits the church rather than himself. That surprises even the most annoying skeptic who finds it hard to fuss about suggested improvements that benefit the congregation. Contentment boosts credibility.

The belittling pastor, however, who chides the church for what it does not do for him or his family usually finds it extremely difficult to lead a congregation into significant change. People are slow to follow a complainer.

The formula, then, for achievement goes like this: contentment + thought-out proposed change = willingness to change. Commit to contentment as a prerequisite for change.

**Step 3: "Re-vision" Your Mission**
Why does the church exist and why are you in the ministry? Those are probing questions that help "re-vision" ministry for oneself and the church. Serious answers to these questions unleash the power of purpose. If the church is to thrive rather than merely survive, our practices and priorities must

be consistent with our vision. A worthwhile, clearly understood purpose frees a church from paralytic passivity.

The church's reason for being—an understandable purpose that links mind, motivation, and muscle—is easily lost in the hubbub of ministry. Perhaps the declining involvement of laity is rooted in unclear purpose; they just do not see the point in much of the church's contemporary efforts. Or an unclear mission may be why congregations tenaciously clutch traditional methods as the only way to do ministry. Stubborn allegiance to conventional methodology and decreasing interest in church activity may be deadly symptoms forcing us to seriously rethink the way we articulate our purpose and mission. The pressing issue in implementing vision is why does the church exist.

Mission and vision belong together and greatly influence each other. Anglican priest Leonard Griffith warns, "If the church ever drops the word mission from its vocabulary, it will have written its own obituary, and its buildings will be like war memorial museums, related to the past but not to the present or the future."[2]

An uncomplicated process for "re-visioning" ministry according to purpose is to "begin with the end in mind."[3] Think how charged up an individual's ministry becomes when he plans it in light of what he wants to accomplish. Consider how this end-in-view concept helps a pastor keep all ministry centered on mission. It brings God into the details of church life as the leader intentionally seeks to understand what He wants done in this particular situation and at this specific time.

Stephen R. Covey, the secular management specialist, helps us more thoroughly understand the value of a crystallized purpose, "People from every walk of life—doctors, academicians, actors, politicians, business professionals, athletes, and plumbers—often struggle to achieve a higher income, more recognition, or a certain degree of professional competence, only to find that their drive to achieve their goal blinded them to the things that really mattered most and now are gone."[4]

Could it be that feelings of futility among Christian workers come from giving too much of oneself for too long to what does not really matter? Perhaps some pastoral stress is rooted in being too active to be really effective. When the vision for the task is obscure, out of focus, or mistaken it is easy to consume enormous energy on useless struggles and unproductive actions.

To return to what really matters, try to "re-vision" your task. Write a purpose statement that incorporates your most compelling purpose for ministry, your goals and timetable for them, and to what causes you are willing to commit vast amounts of personal energy. Then use this purpose statement to control your ministry and life. Lead the church to be mission driven.

## Step 4: Choose Abundance Mentality

The term "abundance mentality" comes from Covey,[5] but its application in the church is as old as the New Testament. Jesus taught over and over again that His little band of weak, spiritually blinded followers could transform their world because of His profuse provisions for them. The Lord intended their scarcity to remind them of His abundance.

Abundance mentality simply means that for everyone there is sufficient grace, faith, victory, provision, good results, creativity, imagination, and accomplishment. None of these provisions has a limited supply. This idea is not intended to encourage or support a "name it and claim it" theology, but it does insist that God's provision is bigger and more abundant than we allow ourselves to believe.

Conversely, the all-too-common scarcity supposition—the precise opposite of abundance mentality—presumes that only one church can succeed in a town or denomination, that there is a limited supply of prospects for the Gospel, and that competition is built-in between pastors because everyone cannot be Number One.

An example of scoffing at the scarcity supposition in secular society is the retail developer who builds three fast-food restaurants in the same block. All three flourish, much to an outsider's amazement. One marketing expert explains, "They feed off each other's success." That's abundance mentality.

Scarcity thinking has lots of churches strangled by tight budgets, falling attendance, and past failures. This survival way of reasoning shows vividly in their perspective, planning, and methods. They suppose, erroneously, that there is only so much money to go around, people only give limited time for ministry, and the community is not interested in their little church. Vision, imagination, and hope are choked to death by scarcity reasoning.

Surprisingly, people who usually think about abundance often resurrect scarcity reasoning when they walk through the church door. Many with responsible jobs and beautiful homes think the church should be the plainest of all meeting spaces with spartan furnishings and austere equipment.

Abundance mentality, on the other hand, believes God wants to bless His people in every situation and that there is enough of His enablement to make every congregation succeed. It believes there are more successes in ministry for those who move forward with initiative and dependence on God than for those who are afraid to risk living on the cutting edge.

Make-do facilities and "just having church" are symptoms of scarcity mentality. The other side of the story is illuminated by a missionary's experience. During the years of the Great Depression, a young woman went as a missionary to Africa to open a specialized ministry to teenage girls. This mission effort became so effective that additional facilities were needed, but no money was available. The young missionary wrote to her mission superior stationed in another country complaining about her deplorable working conditions. In a few days the superior wrote back, "Daughter of the King, if you do not like your conditions, change them. Your Father is rich."

It is true, isn't it?

Most ministry settings have severe limitations which could condition a pastor to choose scarcity reasoning. But take another look; if conditions seem limiting, they can be changed with the Father's help.

The issue is not how little we have, but how much our Father has to give. The potential resources for a fulfilled ministry may be at our finger tips, but we miss it because we live by scarcity suppositions rather than abundance mentality.

### Step 5: Cultivate a Break-Out Spirit

Imagination and innovation are in short supply everywhere, especially in the church. For some unknown reason, many church members want things to remain like they have always been—as if that were possible. Such a hold-the-line posture does not square with reality because the essential nature of both a human being and a church is to change, adapt, and grow. The new keeps ganging up on the old.

Christian history, particularly near the dawn of the early church, offers many examples of persons who took the Gospel in maverick ways to their times. Methods or patterns of action were not sacrosanct to them. Most often, however, they did not try fresh approaches for the sake of newness, but because archaic ways no longer worked. Circumstances and failures often crowded them to break out of old ways of thinking and doing.

This break-out spirit can be seen in the long pilgrimage of faith. For example, the decision to choose the first group of lay leaders in the early church came about because the disciples could not meet the increasing demands of the assistance program for needy widows. They solved the problem in a new way which became the foundation of all shared leadership between clergy and laity. That decision provided a partnership in ministry that was completely new to their way of thinking.

Nationality prejudice was the order of the day until Peter went to the house of Cornelius and found himself declaring, "God does not show favoritism" (Acts 10:34). From that day until now, the church has been struggling to tear down walls of separation between people groups. Even old stick-in-the-mud Peter broke out of his traditional patterns of thinking to open the church doors to people of all origins.

Luther forever changed the heart of Christianity when, after drawing close to God, he saw things in a whole new light. Luther's break-out spirit first sought the mind of God and then asked persistent questions of his environment. He sought demanding cures and applied them to himself, his church, and his world. As a result of his break-out spirit, he became a Christian revolutionary that renewed the church, taking her back — or was it forward — to the authority of the Bible.

Wesley sharpened his break-out spirit when he applied the Gospel to problems in his society and started the Methodist movement, which continues to impact the world to this day. Like all break-out leaders in the history of Christendom, Wesley intersected personal faith, needs of the times, and the power of the Gospel.

Such a break-out spirit requires pastors to be proactive in ministry, a trait few have observed firsthand in the church. From the world of business, Robert J. Kriegel offers an observation about being proactive that applies to churches, "Research shows that the overwhelming majority of Americans (85 percent) are reactive and static, not action- or dynamic- or instinct-oriented. They wait and meet, meet and wait. With a ready arsenal of conservative, conventional wisdom at their disposal, they try to control outcomes in an out-of-control world."[6]

Proactive means taking initiative to find solutions, to make things happen, and to make the church more influential in the lives of the people it serves. Initiative is the key ingredient. That should not be too hard to accomplish because human beings were created to be active rather than reactive and to solve problems rather than be overwhelmed by them.

A useful way to start is to try to think like a beginner again, like you did before you were burdened by experience, expertise, success, or the necessity to defend your position. The challenge, then, is to live out your imagination, vision, and conscience and resist the impact of your conditioning, failure, and disappointments. Stress goes down and hope goes up when a pastor realizes he does not have to be at the mercy of his setting or history.

Every church setting where ministry is offered in the Lord's name needs someone to break out of existing conditions and procedures. Circumstances are too often used to explain why nothing can be done. Break-out people need to create new circumstances, and thousands of environments for ministry need to be transformed rather than accepted. Too many ministries and churches have run out of gas and come to a complete standstill because a leader accepts things the way they are.

Many, however, are afraid of their break-out spirit, so they wait for others to correct situations and improve environments; but those they wait for often do not even see the problem. An achieve-nothing gridlock results.

The Serenity Prayer helps pastors boldly respond to their own break-out spirit: "God, grant me the serenity to accept the things I cannot change, the courage to change the things I can and, the wisdom to know the difference." That second phrase—"the courage to change the things I can"—needs substantially more attention than it is commonly given in the local parish. The break-out spirit in us must replace nonchalant compliance with resolute competence so that situations which victimize pastors can be transformed into golden opportunities for the Gospel.

Secular management specialist John Akers' advice to business speaks loud and clear to pastors, "The people who are playing it totally safe are never going to have either the fun or the reward of the people who decide to take risks, stick out from the crowd, do it differently."[7]

**Step 6: Question Quality vs. Quantity Myth**
False choices in ministry need not be made between quality and quantity because they are inexorably tied together. Ministry usually gets bigger when it gets better.

Think how the two are linked in the business world. Quality determines how many cars General Motors sells on what time table at what cost. Quality of service, on-time arrivals and departures, and safety of aircraft regulate how many passengers fly with an airline. Construction quality affects how many houses a building contractor builds in a year. And quality of material, style, and price largely stimulates the volume of clothing purchases.

Since quality affects quantity on many levels of human existence, it should be no surprise that a pastor's stress is increased by outside forces that expect him to increase attendance and improve the church's influence. Quality and quantity are simply professional expectations that people in many vocations have for themselves; in fact, they would be surprised that anyone thought it should be otherwise.

Many simple steps of improved quality are always possible. Nearly every church, regardless of size or location, can immediately improve quality in some way. As a result, improvement in one area creates an awareness and a commitment to improvement in other areas. In this process, the next step of quality becomes easier than the first. In some astounding, almost imperceptible way, every attempt at quality encourages, or perhaps empowers, a church to move up the spiral of improvement and growth.

A subtle crunch in this line of reasoning comes when pastor and church provide quality ministry and yet attendance drops. Perhaps the answer is like a blue chip stock's value which does not grow every day; quality may always produce immediate increases, but growth usually come over the long haul. If there is no quantity result from quality ministry, the leader should evaluate the quality.

A pastor only increases his frustration if he thinks someone is chasing him with a demand for increased numbers; a glance over his shoulder might reveal it is a self-imposed expectation. Who makes these demands? The problem may be in our heads.

Furthermore, an overarching and sobering statistical reality must also be faced. Most American evangelical churches must not be too serious about the numbers of new converts because more church members are traded across denominational lines than are won.

There is another dimension to the quality issue which is often overlooked. Leading people to Christ invigorates ministry. Pastors who effectively introduce people to Christ are among the most fulfilled people on earth. They know from experience that, like love and marriage and food and fullness, quality and quantity cannot be separated.

The Lord Jesus, our flawless model for all ministry, practiced both quality and quantity. He counted 12 disciples, 120 at Pentecost, and 5,000 men (not counting women and children) as being present at the miraculous breaking of bread and fish. In all these situations, He offered quality ministry but at the same time counted the people.

A few hundred pastors could rid themselves of this draining inner menace if they could come to terms with the reality that they need not choose between quality and quantity. Bona fide quality in ministry means more people become interested in what the church has to offer them—Christ.

Why not free yourself from the numbers game by recommitting to the basic motivation that initially drew you into ministry? Do ministry competently. Make your quality and quantity plans specific, measurable, and time-related.

### Step 7: Transform Ambiguities into Authenticities
The church's prominent ministries of words—preaching and teaching—presuppose that language shapes attitudes, actions, and achievements in the speaker as well as the hearer. Therefore, disheartened pastors need to be extremely careful about what they say to those they love and lead.

Preaching, in many situations, has succeeded in conditioning laypersons to believe the profound thoughts and doctrines about God are too complicated for ordinary people to comprehend. And if people hear that reasoning often enough, it eventually makes them believe Scripture is too difficult for them to understand.

Regarding ambiguities, contemporary churchmen have four

communication impediments that have probably grown out of their training or their common practices:

(1) professional language – technical vocabulary that speaks clearly to theologians, Bible scholars, and fellow pastors;

(2) insider language, sometimes known as King James' speech – that is wonderfully familiar and generally understood by believers but sounds like a foreign tongue to those outside the church;

(3) pop psychological language – jargon which describes phobias, aggression, obsessions, compulsions, co-dependency, and anxieties in place of clearly articulated demands and Christ-provided solutions found in Holy Scripture; and

(4) empty speech – words calculated to sound impressive but say nothing.

The ministry, like other occupations, has *professional language* that may communicate rich meaning to the profession but is meaningless to laypeople. Medicine is a striking example of a technical vocabulary where diseases have long names, body parts have strange-sounding designations, and prescription drugs have two hard-to-pronounce labels, generic and trade. The pastor's technical list includes such terms as neo-orthodoxy, incarnation, predestination, revelation, and theism. Then the scholarly Bible preacher, without meaning to do so, complicates communication when he mentions his research in Greek, his thorough exegesis, and his studies in the history of Christian thought. The end result is a communication disaster that keeps secular people from trying to understand the Gospel.

Why be astonished, then, when a junior high physical education teacher, mechanic, or policewoman tells us they do not understand preaching?

*Insider language* like "being saved" is precious to saints, but it has no meaning to the person outside the church. The hymns and Gospel choruses are full of examples of insider language like "wonderful grace of Jesus," "break Thou the bread of life," "He hideth my soul in the cleft of the rock," and "Sun of my soul."

No one inside the church wants to give up on these beloved phrases, and we shouldn't. But if the purpose of language is to produce understanding, then the man and woman on the street need someone to interpret religious language when they go to church. Otherwise, they consider the church to be an irrelevant relic.

*Pop psychological jargon* rolls like the mighty Jordan from contemporary pulpits. Much of it is neither good psychology nor accurate theology. In a mistaken attempt to be relevant, the preacher uses these self-help terms without judging them against Scripture. Meanwhile, the Gospel keeps telling us that our only real help is in God alone.

Alan Jones, an Anglican pastor, highlights the issue, "One of the things I dread is finding myself terminally ill and being trapped by an eager, young, therapeutically orientated, and humorless clergyman, who will walk all over my psyche by insisting on my sharing my feelings when all I want are the traditional ministrations of prayer and Scripture."[8]

Good psychology and good theology have much common ground, but shallow fads that focus the proclamation of the church on popular psychology rather than on biblical truth leave hearers emotionally confused and spiritually lean.

*Empty speech,* thin verbal communication, presents still another problem. This is well exemplified by the hard-of-hearing saint who was escorted to the front row of a church to hear a famous preacher. After about five minutes of high-sounding palaver, the older woman said in what she thought was a whisper, "He hasn't said anything yet, has he?" Too many pastors preach a bushel of niceties mixed with a bit of technical theological jargon and then send people out to face another week of struggle.

Plain speech, eternal truth, and logic on fire release the Gospel's authentic life-changing power. It is not the foolishness of preaching that people have discarded, but foolish preaching. The old saint knew the score when she shouted from the congregation to her pastor, "Make it plain, brother; make it plain." Nobody needs any more religious double-talk, but many may be ready for a life-changing word from the Lord that they can truly understand.

## Step 8: Cherish People

A veteran pastor lectured beginners: "You can't learn ministry in commentaries, classrooms, or cloisters. All three help, but flesh-and-blood human beings are the raw material of ministry just as the human body is the basic element of medicine. You only learn ministry among people." And he is right on target.

There is no way around it. God intends ministry for people — not for pastors, denominations, theological systems, or social action. The genuinely fulfilled pastor authentically loves people even though they often surprise him. They are the reason Christ came. Their heart for ministry is what provides millions of hours of volunteer service every week for the cause of Christ. People make life both fulfilling and frustrating for pastors.

God's strategy is for a very human vessel called the "pastor" to take the Good News into the fabric of people's lives. In the process of nurturing people, the pastor must remember that regardless of age, appearance, or gender, they are tender, sensitive, and often lonely. In spite of calloused exteriors, gentle feelings and nervous concerns reside inside.

Ministry, therefore, always needs the Common Harry Test. Common Harry is a tenth-grade high school dropout who runs a plumbing shop in everyone's town; he knows ordinary life well but has almost no interest in theoretical reasoning. He needs ministry and he knows it. In the losses and uncertainties of his life, he cannot get along without the good news of the Gospel. And if he can understand ministry, so can everyone else in the typical congregation.

Everything the pastor proposes and plans should pass the Common Harry Test. Will it help Harry? Will it make Harry's life better? Will Harry understand it? Will Harry support it? People like Harry are the reason Christ came and the reason He calls the likes of us to minister.

Much frustration of ministry is rooted in a pastor's being physically or emotionally isolated from people. Sometimes he may be scared or bored by them. Other times he may be outright hostile to them. Some pastoral trainers emphasize how irritating people can be. As a result, beginning pastors sometimes suspect people and give them bad vibes. One pastor admitted, "I have been treating people as though they were lucky to have me. But now I see it is my privilege to serve them in Jesus' name."

Every congregation has difficult people, and some churches have many. But when the pastor is tied with cords of Christian affection to a congregation of generous, devoted, loving people, even the worst tribulations of ministry are bearable.

## Step 9: Fuel Perseverance with Passion

Someone correctly observed, "The main problem of ministry is that pastors give up a minute, a week, or a month too soon."

It is a fact of ministry that achievement often results from a fairly long process of doing the right thing for the right reason. And though many pastors believe and preach perseverance, they frequently detest it because of its exacting and continuous demands.

Gritting your teeth, doing your duty, and pushing yourself to do what you do not want to do one more time is the popular concept of perseverance. This notion believes achievement results from doggedly hammering away at a task. So in many minds, perseverance is high on obligation and low on enjoyment.

Perseverance, however, has a more attractive but seldom discussed dimension—an intense, passionate commitment to a cause or task that turns work into fun. Fired-up pastors do not have to force themselves to work. Passionate perseverance rekindles motivation, so ministry is a joy instead of a job, a delight instead of a drag, an ecstacy instead of an obligation. Interestingly, it often splashes over into marriage and parenting.

Passion produces perseverance. O.J. Simpson, the football great, explains, "When you're excited about what you are doing, you'll practice more, and you won't see it as work at all . . . it's all part of the game."[9] His idea works in pastorates too.

Passion for ministry often makes it possible for a pastor to sail right past many risks. Advice directed to business leaders applies to pastors too: "If your passion for the project [ministry] is lower than a 7 on a scale of 10, either change it, get yourself more fired up, or forget it. It's too tough out there and there's too much on your plate already to take on something you are not genuinely excited about. A project under a 7 will become a burden to you and your people, and you'll only go through the motions with it."[10]

Passionate perseverance makes ministry more interesting; impacts those around us; and increases our own stability, resiliency, and buoyancy.

## Step 10: Treasure the Pleasure of God

Inspiration for achieving balance in ministry shines through the story of Eric Liddell, the famous British track star who became a gold medalist in the 1924 Olympics. When interviewed about his successful race, Liddell said, "When I am running, I feel the pleasure of God."[11]

Balance, a key concept for healthy ministry, is difficult to achieve because it requires striving with the neverending demands placed upon pastors. Often it all seems like a circus juggler's act.

The collision of roles and expectations in the pastorate reminds us of a time when a frightening onset of dizziness sent one of us to a physician, expecting to receive sophisticated tests and elaborate treatment. Medical laypeople have imaginations about the onset of strokes, high blood pressure, or Méniere's disease. But the doctor offered a surprisingly simple suggestion: "Whenever you feel dizzy, just look at something straight — like a door jam — for a few seconds; then you'll be able to function." Though that office visit cost plenty, it gave simple insight for times when pastoring seems confusing: to keep in balance, look at something straight.

What a useful combination for increasing satisfaction in ministry—*feel the pleasure of God* and *look at something straight*. Taken together, these ideas sound like Hebrews 12:2, "Let us fix our eyes on Jesus, the author and perfecter of our faith, who for the joy set before Him endured the cross, scorning its shame, and sat down at the right hand of the throne of God."

In an ultimate sense, it is God whom the pastor must please with a balanced life and a fruitful ministry. And He sometimes defines balance and fruitfulness differently than we do. Be assured that God is always satisfied with our best effort. He knows every detail of our lives and ministries, and He is a thousand times easier to please than most of us think.

This inner call for balance takes us back to the unrealistic expectation issue, which sometimes starts with the pastor himself. Admittedly, everyone in the pastor's sphere of influence, including his mother who lives 2,000 miles away, has an opinion about how he should do his work. No two evaluations agree, not even the pastor's and his spouse's. So joy for the work is not likely to flow from other people. Thus, the minister must determine what ministry is to be for him.

To feel the pleasure of God in ministry—what a liberating thought in the midst of so many contemporary risks. Sadly, many pastors rush through life without once realizing that their work is pleasing to the Chief.

**Step 11: Dare to Lead**
No one can give a pastor leadership of a church by a one-time appointment or election. Two monumental stumbling blocks prevent it: (1) leadership is always earned and never bestowed, and (2) no one follows those who do not lead. No call, contract, credential, or ecstatic religious experience makes an individual a leader. The most impressive and magnetic characteristic of the effective pastor/leader is single-minded devotion to lead the people into the deeper depths of Christlikeness.

This non-bestowal leadership concept is sometimes hard for pastors to accept because they are called by God, set apart for ministry by ordination, and formally installed by a congregation or ecclesiastical official. Then the bestowed idea is mistakenly reinforced from the first Sunday when members of the congregation begin calling him "Reverend" or "Pastor."

However, a church assignment or a formal rank only means the pastor has permission or authority to begin earning leadership. A call to a church is a call to get to work. A wise denominational administrator counseled a green pastor, "Now that you have been invited to pastor a group of people, it means they expect you to lead. If you are to be a leader, you have to earn it after you officially become the pastor." The high cost of earning genuine pastoral leadership requires one to take ministry into the details of people's lives.

Pastors who think appointment, election, or ordination makes them leaders are often bewildered because no one follows them. In those circumstances, ministers need to examine their pastoral care of the flock of God. No pastor has really led until he applies the Spirit of Christ to every dimension of church life, including efficient organization, solid business principles, strong preaching, and sound theology. None of these is adequate without the Spirit of Christ.

That essential element of applying the Spirit of Christ to all dimensions of the work helps everyone's commitment to improve from passing interest to increased intensity. Then clergy and laity are able to move from arm's length suspicion to wholehearted confidence so they can work together like a masterful symphony orchestra.

Peter Drucker offers insightful guidance to the church when he calls leadership a peak performance by one who is "the trumpet that sounds a clear sound of the organization's goals." His five requirements for this task are amazingly reliable and useful for those who dare to lead churches:

(1) a leader works;

(2) a leaders sees his assignment as responsibility rather than rank or privilege;

(3) a leader wants strong, capable, self-assured, independent associates;

(4) a leader creates human energies and vision;

(5) a leader develops followers' trust by his own consistency and integrity.[12]

By using Drucker's leadership directives, a creative surge of satisfaction can come to a pastor. He is then able to harness energy which has been previously wasted. Consequently, both congregational achievement and pastoral fulfillment follow just as day follows night.

To have an unquestioned right to lead, a pastor must activate these directives in the depths of his own personhood and practice them in the details of the church's work. Strong, capable people stand in the wings in many churches waiting to follow a competent, Christlike leader who dares to lead them to accomplish worthwhile objectives.

## Step 12: Exegete Your Environment

Good sermons require reliable exegesis. Exegetical labor, when faithfully done, helps a preacher discover a biblical writer's meaning and bring truth into trustworthy dialogue with contemporary life. This work is never complete until it transfers what has been learned about the text into words hearers understand, whatever their level of sophistication or academic achievement.

Effective biblical preaching is a continuous interplay between the meaning of Scripture, the needs of hearers, and the character and competence of the preacher. Expositor Alexander Maclaren cogently abridged the idea, "A true sermon always has humanity within it and Divinity behind it."[13] Exegesis allows Scripture to illuminate and examine and revolutionize real people who live in the contemporary world.

One trainer of preachers suggests the task of hermeneutics is to bridge the differences of time, place, culture, and meaning between the biblical writer and the modern hearer—the preacher connects the two.

However, another set of slightly different exegetical skills is highly important to equip a pastor to understand, overcome, or make use of existing risks. This essential skill is the life-long commitment and quest by a pastor to exegete his world—himself, his family, his congregation, his denomination, his town, and his culture—so the pastor develops a thoroughly accurate awareness of the unique dimensions of his assignment.

This new exegetical skill is a commitment to discovering and rediscovering the subtleties of the environment where ministry is to be done and then using that information to shape the details of ministry.

Exegeting the environment for ministry means making a positive Gospel response to the conditions and demands of a particular situation. It means asking exegetical questions about the setting: What does this mean? Is my view correct? What do I know about this issue from other settings? Who is in charge? What are they saying? What is happening in my small corner of the world?

For a pastor, it is a lethal delusion to assume every situation is like the previous one, just as it is a miscalculation to suppose a specific setting remains static. Nothing could be more inaccurate. Settings of ministry, like a mountain stream, may look the same year after year, but they are in a constant flux of change; the familiar appearance is deceiving. No two ministry settings are twins. Little is like it used to be, nor will it ever be just like it is again.

The letters H.B. receives at Focus on the Family are filled with distressing disappointment. Some of that is unnecessary because it grows out of a pastor's inability to understand himself in his surroundings. Many are immensely frustrated because they try to do their ministry in the same way in every setting—a kind of one-year effort done over forty years in several churches.

Serving an old established church that has been spiritually abused by a previous pastor is very different from gathering people together in a new church plant. In each church, the pastor needs to exegete its distinct differences and the congregation's way of looking at its task. Neither church will flourish if the pastor does not make use of these variations.

The minister's family situation affects ministry too. The beginning pastor with preschool children and a working wife does ministry differently than one whose children are teenagers or one whose nest is empty. Exegeting distinguishing characteristics in his own family helps a pastor cope with, respond to, or enjoy the unique qualities of his marriage and family. And it also helps him understand the home situations of his parishioners.

Think too of denominational and doctrinal differences. The pastor who serves an independent congregational church has a much different situation than the pastor who serves in a denominational structure. Many clergy leaders find themselves facing many obstacles when they do not factor these issues into their ministry.

Tools for exegeting the environment include: awareness, sensitivity, reflection, and listening, as well as historical records and key questions of knowledgeable persons in the congregation and community.

Exegeting the environment requires a pastor to know more about his community than anyone else. Pastor Rick Warren of Saddleback Community Church in Southern California advocates, "You cannot reach people unless you understand them first."[14] And he insists that nothing can take the place of a pastor interviewing 200 or more unchurched people to find out what they think about the church and the community.

Further, George Hunter III, dean of the E. Stanley Jones School of Evangelism at Asbury Seminary, advises that a pastor get intimately acquainted with his environment for ministry by discovering who lives in the community and why, what they think, and how they act. He also suggests interviews with school officials, marketing people, regional planning personnel, and human services providers in the community.[15]

Some pastors might profit from college or university courses in the social sciences such as sociology, anthropology, cross-cultural communication, or marriage and family — making up for blind spots in their training and catching up in quickly changing fields.

Modern prophets like Chuck Colson of Prison Fellowship fame must be heeded, "I believe that today in the West, and particularly in America, the new barbarians are all around us. They are not hairy Goths and Vandals, swilling fermented brew and ravishing maidens; they are not Huns and Visigoths storming our borders or scaling our city walls. No, this time the invaders have come from within."[16]

How sad for a pastor to be crippled in ministry because he does not know how to exegete the rich treasures of Holy Scripture. But it is equally tragic not to be able to understand one's times.

## THE CONTEMPORARY CHALLENGE
## TAKE CHARGE OF YOUR MINISTRY NOW

These twelve steps will refocus your attention away from the contemporary crises to enormous opportunities at your elbow, down the street, or across the world. These steps offer handles to help you redemptively respond to the most astounding possibilities ever experienced by the Christian church.

Never in human history were pastors more needed than now. In a time when personal and public sins have strangled satisfaction out of life, there is a crying need for someone like a pastor to put broken people in touch with the Author of authentic wholeness. In this period of international despair when civic officials admit social pathologies cannot be remedied with government programs and expenditures, someone like you is needed to proclaim the reforming work of Christ for individuals, communities, and cultures. At a time when loneliness and isolation have reached epidemic proportions, a pastor can offer spiritually homeless persons a different status in the family of God. These times demand that pastors root and ground people in the new life realities of Scripture and stimulate their appetites for a personal faith in Christ.

231

All these mammoth miseries offer unparalleled possibilities for kingdom builders. How exciting to realize that God has placed pastors in the middle of the action as agents of reconciliation, hope, and righteousness.

This is a daring, demanding day for everyone commissioned by our Lord to teach, preach, and lead. Let's seize and use it.

Because ministry to impact these times will be diverse, complicated, and creative, it is impossible to describe all the ways a pastor might renew himself and fall in love again with his calling. If ministry, however, is viewed as a work of art to impact all who experience it, then these twelve steps can be used as paint and canvas and brushes and lessons in texture and color. But nothing in any book could faintly substitute for divine guidance, renewed passion for souls, fired up perseverance, Christ-inspired imagination, or sacrificial resourcefulness.

Both these puzzling times and the Gospel call us to give it our best—one more time. Don't wait for a surge of courage to start again. Get up and get going. Then courage, energy, and creativity will follow you into the pulpit, stand by your side in the dark midnights, strengthen you when you want to quit, and follow you home to reassure you that you can do it again tomorrow.

Keep close company with God by praying Frances Ridley Havergal's prayer:

Let me then be always growing,
    Never, never standing still;
Listening, learning, better knowing
    Thee and Thy most blessed will.

Pastors are at risk, but there is good news. This book is a corporate testimony that there is help for pastors and hope for the church. Ministry thrives in such perplexing times because that is where God's enablement works best in the details of ministry.

# Fall In Love Again
# with Your Calling

Ministry is madness unless you love it. These days, pastors are overstressed by soul-crushing burdens. Many ministers are seriously considering separations or divorces from their calling because they feel so fatigued and empty. Yesterday's idealism has corroded in their souls. The fires of passion for the pastorate are burning low.

As the church looks forward to the twenty-first century and faces intimidating and increasing chaos, lay leaders, pastors, and church systems should consider if and how it might be possible for weary, disheartened pastors to fall in love again with their calling.

*Pastors at Risk* candidly identifies and examines the multifaceted hazards that have caused and multiplied the prevailing crises. The overall picture is not pretty or inspiring. The skies are dark, the winds are blowing with gale force, and the storm may get much worse.

But the world needs pastors now more than ever.

When the romance for ministry burns low, how can a pastor fall in love again with his calling? As a beginning, he might recall five rudimentary realities that appear over and over in the pages of *Pastors at Risk:*

(1) God trusts you. What a revolutionary idea! God demonstrated His confidence in you when He called you. His call shows you have the raw materials to flourish in ministry. In His wisdom, He knew you have the stamina and vigor to face these times. The exact moment in human history when God intends for your ministry to thrive may not be a good time to abandon ship.

(2) Ministry is at the center of all the action that matters. It is the arena for fulfillment and meaning. There is nothing like it anywhere. Like no other profession, the pastor's day-by-day work takes him into the victories and heartaches of people's lives and everything in between.

Who else has a commission from God to walk into the main events of the human drama as a proxy for the living Christ? Who would willingly avoid such an exciting place if they could? Ministry is where the real action is.

(3) Intimacy with Christ fuels constructive ministry. At the heart of ministry stands a secret that is being rediscovered with exhilarating frequency these days. The secret is out in the open—no one is able to do authentic ministry without an intimate first name relationship with the living Lord. Without intimate companionship with Christ, ministry is only an empty effort. Perhaps the highest privilege of being a pastor is the opportunity and pure joy of living in close contact with Christ.

(4) Marriage and family stability strengthens ministry. For too long, the pastor's spouse and family have been viewed as a competitive or adversarial factor against effective ministry. The idea is absurd. It's time to cherish the pastor's family and home as a place of renewal, sanctuary, and peace. Consequently, the affection, emotional energy, and time he invests in the most significant people in his life enriches his ministry. His commitment to family makes him better as a fulfilled Christ-centered human being.

(5) Perplexing times provide growth opportunities. Tough circumstances force us to depend fully on the benefit of God's power. In response to our dependency, God transforms our

obstacles into accomplishments. Then, divine enablement helps us achieve heroic accomplishments even as it nourishes us into great souls. The Father's enablement is real. Many of the kingdom's most notable victories have been achieved in the most difficult settings.

*Pastors at Risk* does not intend to shame anyone into continuing ministry for the wrong reasons. Neither does it aim to encourage anyone to leave the pastorate. The goal is to trigger a groundswell that encourages pastors everywhere to reinvent ministry for troubled times.

We hope every pastor and his spouse will know how cherished and needed they are for renewing the cause of Christ in the world.

We want every clergy couple to have the most adventuresome marriage in the congregation they lead.

We challenge every pastor and his wife to make home a happy haven for the children.

We call every pastor and spouse to do more with their money and to do ministry so well that lay leaders are eager to raise their salary.

We urge every pastor to find a new intimacy with Christ so his life reflects personal holiness and so that all he does is blessed from a close connection with our Lord.

And we desire for every pastor to enjoy emotional and spiritual health so stress and burnout will become extinct among pastors.

We pray and hope that every pastor will rekindle a fervent love affair with ministry.

Why not fall in love again with your calling? Love a world that needs you so badly. Love people who make up your church family. Love the enchantments and fascination and ambiguities of ministry. Even try to love the demands that dark days bring.

A trustworthy cornerstone for rekindling this love affair and for reinventing ministry for trouble times comes from the Apostle Paul, "Since through God's mercy we have this ministry, we do not lose heart" (2 Cor. 4:1).

DR. JAMES C. DOBSON is Founder and President of Focus on the Family, a nonprofit organization that produces a nationally syndicated radio program heard daily on more than 1,450 stations.

For fourteen years he was an Associate Clinical Professor of Pediatrics at the University of Southern California School of Medicine, and he served seventeen years on the Attending Staff of Children's Hospital of Los Angeles in the Divisions of Child Development and Medical Genetics.

His many best-selling books include
*Dare to Discipline*
*Parenting Isn't for Cowards*
*Hide or Seek*
*The Strong-Willed Child*
*Love Must Be Tough*
*Love for a Lifetime*

ARCHIBALD D. HART is currently Professor and Dean of the Graduate School of Psychology, Fuller Theological Seminary, Pasadena, California. He is a licensed psychologist and specializes in psychotherapy from a Christian orientation, stress management and the use of biofeedback techniques, neuropsychodiagnosis, and cognitive approaches to psychology.
*Unlocking the Mystery of Your Emotions*
*Coping with Depression in Ministry*
*Children of Divorce*
*The Hidden Link Between Adrenalin and Stress*
*Healing Adult Children of Divorce*

JERRY BRIDGES is Vice-president for Corporate Affairs of The Navigators, Colorado Springs, Colorado. He combines a Bible teaching ministry with his corporate responsibilities for The Navigators.

He is author of five books:
*The Pursuit of Holiness*
*The Practice of Godliness*
*The Crises of Caring*
*Trusting God*
*Transforming Grace*

GORDON and GAIL MACDONALD have lived in New York City for four years where he has been pastor of Trinity Baptist Church. He previously served congregations in Kansas, Illinois, and Massachusetts. He also served as president of InterVarsity Christian Fellowship. In January of 1993, the congregation of Grace Chapel, Lexington, Massachusetts—where Gordon

**236**

previously served for thirteen years—called him to return to the pulpit ministry there. The MacDonalds moved to Massachusetts in February of 1993. Pastor MacDonald's books are as follows:

*Til the Heart Be Touched* (coauthored with Gail)
*Christ-Followers in the Real World*
*Ordering Your Private World*
*Renewing Your Spiritual Passion*
*Rebuilding Your Broken World*

RON BLUE is the managing partner of Ronald Blue & Co., a financial advisory firm with offices in Atlanta, Orlando, and Indianapolis. He combines professional expertise with a thorough understanding of biblical principles of money management. He's the best-selling author of *Master Your Money* and (with his wife, Judy) *Money Matters for Parents and Their Kids*. He earned his master's in business administration at Indiana University. Blue and his wife live with their five children in Atlanta.

LINDA RILEY has been a pastor's wife for twenty years in Torrance, California. She is the founder and director of Called Together Ministries (CTM)—a resource organization for pastors' wives for learning, inspiration, and fellowship. CTM offers a resource catalog of books and tapes, a quarterly newsletter called "Serving Together," and a peer counseling phone service for clergy families. The Listening Line number is 310-214-2332 and the address is Called Together Ministry, 20820 Avis Avenue, Torrance, California, 90503.

# NOTES

## Chapter 1

1. This phrase is taken from the subtitle of Charles Colson, *Against the Night: Living in the New Dark Ages* (Ann Arbor, Mich.: Servant, 1989).
2. Ibid., 111.

## Chapter 2

1. 1991 Survey of Pastors, Fuller Institute of Church Growth.
2. George Barna, *What Americans Believe* (Ventura, Calif.: Regal, 1991), 24.
3. Ibid., 299.
4. "Is the Pastor's Family Safe at Home?" *Leadership* (Fall 1992): 38–44.
5. Hugh Prather, *Notes on How to Live in the World* (Garden City, N.Y.: Doubleday, 1986), 201–3.
6. William J. Bennett, "Cultural Indicators Chart Our Moral Climate," *Colorado Springs Gazette,* 28 March 1993, Sec. D5.
7. Elizabeth Skoglund, *Beyond Loneliness* (Garden City, N.Y.: Doubleday, 1980), 118.
8. Ibid., 144.

## Chapter 3

1. Quoted in James Hamilton, *The Pair in Your Parsonage* (Kansas City: Beacon Hill, 1982), 10.

## Chapter 4

1. Paul A. Mickey and Ginny W. Ashmore, *Clergy Families: Is Normal Life Possible?* (Grand Rapids: Zondervan, 1991), 17.
2. H. Newton Malony and Richard A. Hunt, *The Psychology of Clergy* (Harrisburg, Pa.: Morehouse, 1991), 9.
3. Ibid., 36.
4. Richard C. Halverson, "Planting Seeds and Watching Them Grow," *Leadership* (Fall 1980): 20.

# Notes

## Chapter 6

1. Mickey and Ashmore, *Clergy Families,* 132.
2. Ron Blue, *The Debt Squeeze* (Pomona, Calif.: Focus on the Family, 1989), 24–25.

## Chapter 8

1. John A. Sanford, *Ministry Burnout* (New York: Paulist Press, 1982), 18.
2. Ibid.
3. Lloyd J. Ogilvie, *Making Stress Work for You* (Waco, Texas: Word, 1984), 125.
4. Ibid., 131.

## Chapter 9

1. Leonard Griffith, *We Have This Ministry* (Waco, Texas: Word, 1973), 16.
2. Robert K. Hudnut, *This People, This Parish* (Grand Rapids: Zondervan, 1986), 19.
3. Henri Nouwen, *Reaching Out* (Garden City, N.Y.: Doubleday, 1975), 97.
4. Ibid.

## Chapter 11

1. Eugene H. Peterson, *Working the Angles* (Grand Rapids: Eerdmans, 1987).
2. Griffith, *This Ministry,* 87.
3. Stephen R. Covey, *The 7 Habits of Highly Effective People* (New York: Simon and Schuster, 1989), 97.
4. Ibid., 98.
5. Ibid., 219.
6. Robert J. Kriegel, *If It Ain't Broke . . . Break It!* (New York: Warner, 1991), 85.
7. Ibid., 169.
8. Alan Jones, *Sacrifice and Delight: A Spirituality for Ministry,* (San Francisco: Harper, 1992), 34.
9. *Forbes,* 2 October 1989, 31.

10. Kriegel, *If It Ain't Broke,* 15.
11. Ibid., 19.
12. Peter F. Drucker, *Managing for the Future* (New York: Dutton, 1992), 119–23.
13. A.W. Blackwood, *Expository Preaching for Today* (Nashville: Abingdon, 1953), 25.
14. George Hunter III, *How to Reach Secular People* (Nashville: Abingdon, 1992), 154.
15. Ibid., 155.
16. Colson, *Against the Night,* 23.